MENSA

ASSESS YOURSELF

THIS IS A CARLTON BOOK

Text and puzzle content copyright © British Mensa Limited 1998
Design and artwork copyright © Carlton Books Limited 1998

This edition published by Carlton Books Limited 1998

A CIP catalogue for this book is available from the British Library.

ISBN 1-85868-538-9

Printed and bound in Italy

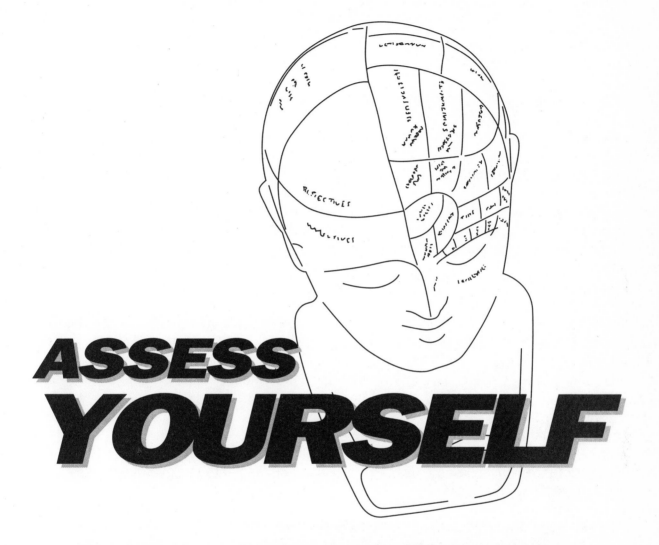

ASSESS YOURSELF

The Mensa guide to evaluating your emotions, skills, strengths and weaknesses

Robert Allen

CARLTON

AMERICAN MENSA LTD.

American Mensa Ltd is an organization for individuals who have one common trait: an IQ in the top 2% of the nation. Over 50,000 current members have found out how smart they are. This leaves room for an additional 4.5 million members in America alone. You may be one of them.

Looking for intellectual stimulation?

If you enjoy mental exercise, you'll find lots of good "workout programs" in the *Mensa Bulletin*, our national magazine. Voice your opinion in one of the newsletters published by each of our 150 local chapters. Learn from the many books and publications that are available to you as a member.

Looking for social interaction?

Are you a "people person," or would you like to meet other people with whom you feel comfortable? Then come to our local meetings, parties, and get-togethers. Participate in our lectures and debates. Attend our regional events and national gatherings. There's something happening on the Mensa calendar almost daily. So, you have lots of opportunities to meet people, exchange ideas, and make interesting new friends.

Looking for others who share your special interest?

Whether yours is as common as crossword puzzles or as esoteric as Egyptology, there's a Mensa Special Interest Group (SIG) for it.

Take the challenge. Find out how smart you really are. Contact American Mensa Ltd today and ask for a free brochure. We enjoy adding new members and ideas to our high-IQ organization.

American Mensa Ltd
201 Main Street, Suite 1101
Fort Worth, Texas 76102

Or, if you don't live in the USA and you'd like more details, you can contact:
Mensa International, 15 The Ivories, 628 Northampton Street, London N1 2NY, England
who will be happy to put you in touch with your own national Mensa.

CONTENTS

*t*his is, I have to tell you, not a very respectable book. The reason? It does something that you are never supposed to do, and that is to combine psychometrics with popular psychology. Yet I make no apology for treating the subject in what to psychologists may appear a rather flippant manner. In the first place my information about psychometric personality assessment is accurate and is not in any way mixed with information about less 'respectable' methods. If you are easily offended by anything that is not 'real' psychology then please regard the book as two separate volumes within one cover. The first half contains information, told in what I hope is an accessible, anecdotal and interesting yet accurate manner, about psychometric personality testing. This is important because psychometric testing is rapidly becoming an everyday tool for personnel selection and development. Or, put more brutally, if you want a job or promotion, you're probably going to get tested. It therefore makes sense to understand what testing is, what it does, what it cannot do, and how tests are constructed and administered.

The second half of the book is fun and games. I make no other claims for it, and if you feel that fun and science should not be found within the same covers, then you have every right to that opinion, but you have bought the wrong book. My point is that, on an everyday level, personality assessment goes on all the time. It is an important part of human psychology, and in a purely intuitive way we all do it on a daily basis. Every time we see someone unfamiliar, every time we meet a new acquaintance, every time a new colleague is taken on at the office, everyone concerned forms opinions of that person's personality. Sometimes these opinions will be used for nothing more than fuelling the office gossip machine, but on other occasions they may well be used to make quite important decisions about the person concerned. Take, for example, the police. Do they ask a suspect to complete a psychometric personality test as part of their interrogation? On rare occasions they may, but in the vast majority of cases they rely on gut feeling, hunches, intuition, whatever you want to call it. And the subject of their investigations may go to jail purely on the strength of such hunches. So, though popular personality assessment may be subject to severe disapprobation from the psychological establishment, and even though that disapprobation may be fully justified, it is a fact of life, a thing that people have built into their mental make-up. It does affect the way we live, and therefore I would submit that its place in this book is justified. However, I will at all times keep what I regard as 'popular, intuitive' methods separate from mainstream psychology. Even then I shall be in trouble, for many adherents of graphology, body language, color analysis, etc., regard their methods as at least as successful, if not more so, as those used by psychometricians. You will have the chance to judge for yourself.

Personality assessment, though not necessarily known by that name, is as old as humanity. Because people live in society and because they are bound together by the bonds of competition and cooperation, it has always been important for us to understand each other's personalities. One may well imagine that when our hunter-gatherer ancestors finally cornered a beast they had been pursuing, it would have been of the greatest importance to know which hunter would remain brave when the animal tried to break out, and which would flee. Similarly, the competitive side of human nature requires people to size each other up, look for weaknesses in a rival, and search for the opportunity to come out on top. Courtiers and politicians would have sized each other up trying to decide who, out of a tricky bunch of customers, was the most tricky and who, for the moment at least, might make a useful ally. The number of situations where humans need to understand each other's motives, instincts and likely reactions is almost limitless.

Beyond any real need for information, humans seem to be just plain curious about each other. If you are the type who finds other people interesting, you will doubtless have spent many hours chatting to your friends about the motives, quirks and relationships of other friends or, for that matter, enemies. You will not be surprised to hear that you are far from unique. Most of us do it, and where, for example, would gossip be without a hefty dose of personality assessment? But there is more to it than mere amusement. As communal creatures, the success of our society – indeed, its very survival – is dependent on our constantly assessing and re-assessing each other. Situations change, as do people to a greater or lesser extent, and the results of those changes have effects, trivial or profound, on our communities and societies. It is largely by instinct that we keep ourselves up to date on these matters. In addition to understanding the personalities of others we also have a great need to understand ourselves, and this, to the surprise of many, is an area that people often find extremely difficult. Life presents us with a series of choices that stretches from the cradle (teddy bear or fuzzy rabbit?) to the grave (buried or cremated?). Our whole lives are governed by the choices we make, and those choices will be affected fundamentally by our personality. In employment it will be important to know whether we prefer to work with other people or alone, whether we value money more than status or job satisfaction, whether we like to be outdoors or in an office. Away from work we have to decide who to marry – or, of course, whether to marry – whether to have children, and if so, how many. The list just goes on and on. The rather strange thing is that so many people are very bad at knowing what their own personality is really like. I spend a great deal of time working with people who are experiencing problems at work or in relationships that are, at root, caused by a fundamental ignorance of their own personality. Even stranger is the fact that once you have pointed out to these people what your assessment has discovered, they say, 'Oh yes, that's exactly what I'm like!'

There is much more to self-assessment than purely utilitarian matters. We are actively interested in what we are like. Huge amounts of time are spent in self-analysis of one sort or another. In modern times, and especially since the advent of psychoanalysis, this search for self-knowledge has become almost a plague, and hardly a day passes without some new fad or theory that adds to the already bewildering array. To some extent this may be symptomatic of societies where people are so affluent and have so little concern about how to keep themselves fed and housed that they have enormous leisure for introspection. But that is only a development of an urge that has been with us for thousands of years. Great writers, philosophers, doctors and religious leaders in every country and every era have ventured theories concerning what makes people tick. And such theories have been received with great enthusiasm because deep in our hearts we all think that we are extremely interesting beings and well worth close examination.

Since I have mentioned the early history of personality assessment, we should take a quick look at the history of this art. Let's start with an ancient Greek philosopher called Theophrastus. He wrote a series of sketches entitled *The Characters* in which he included well-known stereotypes such as the Flatterer, the Coward, and so on. His descriptions of these types are completely familiar to us today, and we could all think of people who would fit them. Greek playwrights also dealt with well-known personality types. Greek actors wore masks called *persona* and it is these that give us the word 'personality'. When the audience saw an actor in his mask they knew immediately what to expect of his character. This idea of treating people as types has continued throughout history and surfaces centuries later in the *commedia dell'arte* of the Italian Renaissance with its familiar character types, such as the handsome hero, the sly servant and the jealous husband. We can see it in Hollywood movies, even very modern ones, in which you may still find the Tart with a Heart, for example, who would have been familiar to audiences hundreds of years earlier. Modern TV soap operas also use such characters, and the viewer knows straightaway who represents the nosy neighbor, the pretty young girl, or the villainous trickster.

Nor is this way of regarding personality peculiar to western culture. Japanese drama used masked characters whose features gave the audience an immediate insight into their personality, and traditional Chinese opera used a formal system of make-up that provided the audience with the same information (heroes had a lot of red in their make-up; evil characters had white).

The attempt to assess personality has persisted and has spawned a huge variety of methods – some quite bizarre, and some still having their adherents today. Phrenology, or reading the bumps of the head, was popular in the last century and was seriously considered to reveal inner truths about the subject's personality. Graphology, or the study of handwriting, was, and is, popular. Though widely dismissed by scientists, it is widely practised and given credence by many. In France especially, graphology still commands a considerable amount of respect in some quarters. It is easy to see why. Common sense tells us that something as intimately connected to a person as their handwriting does indeed reveal personality. We have all seen examples that seem 'typical' of a certain person's character. It is when you try to construct a system based on such findings that you discover there is no solid basis for believing that handwriting is indicative of character. In recent times other fads have arisen that claim to be able to indicate personality. Colour analysis was one such which, for a while in the '70s, was considered by some to have something useful to contribute. People were attracted to the idea that a person's choice of colours might be indicative of their personality type. Great theories were constructed in which red became the color of assertiveness, yellow was associated with intellect, and so on. We will take a closer look at some of the more unorthodox methods of personality assessment later.

What of mainstream psychology? What does it have to offer by way of personality assessment? Let's go back for a moment to the types described by Theophrastus. There was an underlying assumption that these held constant over time. The Garrulous Man remained talkative in any company, and whether his conversation was welcome or not. Similarly, the Coward could be relied upon to behave without courage, and the Fool would always be stupid. These types are distantly but quite clearly related to what modern psychologists call 'traits'. It is widely assumed these days that someone who, when tested, shows a marked tendency to be sociable and outgoing will be so regularly and will remain so over time. This will also apply to other traits such as anxiety or creativity. Most of the personality analysis carried out in business and commerce today relies upon 'trait theory' as its basis.

However, there are other theories of personality that we should mention. Those who favor a behavioral approach would say that personality is shaped by our reactions to external circumstances both now and in the past. Others would have us believe that all our actions stem from the promptings of unconscious urges that may be so deeply buried we are completely unaware of them. This is known technically as psychodynamic theory and stems largely from the work of Sigmund Freud. In recent years unconscious urges have been very popular as an explanation for behavior. This has led to some bizarre and even sinister developments. Some psychotherapists, especially in the US, have championed the idea that women who have been sexually abused in childhood bury these traumatic events so deeply in their unconscious that memories of what occurred can only be restored by a period of intense therapy. Women who thought they had had a happy, or at least unexceptional, childhood have been urged to recover the most painful memories of abuse. This has been, unsurprisingly, a very controversial issue. The problem about unconscious urges is that they are unconscious. Who is to arbitrate as to whether they are present and to what extent they are responsible for a person's behavior? Naturally, some psychologists and psychiatrists are anxious to lay claim to this area of expertise. Others are not so sure.

As trait theory is the predominant method in use today, let's examine in some detail how it works. Our old friends the Greeks, not content with classifying dramatic characters, also came up with four main 'types' into which people could be sorted. In about 400BC Hippocrates concluded that people could be sanguine (blood: optimistic, hopeful), phlegmatic (phlegm: apathetic), choleric (bile: irascible), or melancholic (black bile: sad, depressed). So successful were these classifications that they were further developed by Galen in the second century AD and are still familiar to us today. However, the system was too clumsy. People do not fit neatly into one category or another.

That did not prevent later scientists from trying another classification by type, but this time the deciding factor was body shape. This theory was well explained for the layman by the psychologist Eric Berne:

A human being comes from an egg. As that egg develops, it forms a three-layered tube and the three layers develop into different body organs. The inner layer becomes the stomach and lungs, the middle layer into bones, joints, muscles, and blood vessels, and the outer layer into the skin and nervous system. As the embryo develops, these three systems grow about equally and, when the baby is finally born, it will have roughly equal amounts of gut, muscle and brain. However, differences do occur and we can easily observe that some people have a much larger amount of gut, some are noticeably broad and muscular, and others have a more developed brain.

The theory of body types divides these people up according to their physique and gives them names accordingly. The people who are round and fat because they have a more developed gut are called endomorphs, the broad, muscular ones are known as mesomorphs, and the thin, long, ones are known as ectomorphs.

Now comes the tricky bit. According to some writers these types also appear to describe certain people very well, and the fat, jolly man or the broad, muscular, hearty sportsman are types with which we are all familiar. There is also a general feeling that brainy people should be skinny, long and have larger heads. Psychologists, who are very good at making up names for things (even when they are not quite sure that they exist), have invented names for personality types based on body shape. Thus the person whose physique is dominated by the gut is a viscerotonic endomorph. This is what Berne says about this type:

His abdomen is big because he has lots of intestines. He likes to take things in. He likes to take in food, and affection and approval as well. Going to a banquet with people who like him is his idea of a fine time.

The next type is the somatotonic mesomorph. Berne says:

He would rather breathe than eat. He has a bony head, big shoulders, and a square jaw . . . Li'l Abner and other men of action belong to this type. Such men make good lifeguards and construction workers.

The cerebrotonic ectomorph, on the other hand, has a long body shape and thin bones and muscles. 'He looks like an absent-minded professor and often is one,' according to Berne. Such a person is likely to be nervous, jumpy, and not very keen on action. They are much better suited to reflective pursuits than anything else.

Having established this as a theory, can we use it to make predictions about people's behavior? The first and most obvious objection is simply that most people do not fit neatly into any of these categories. I know in my own case that I rather enjoy eating (and my figure suffers for it), I work

with my brain rather than my body, but I also walk, run, cycle and work out at the gym. I'm sure that I am not unique; most of the people you see in any street would be hard to place firmly as any of the three types we have discussed.

Does this theory hold up at all? Does it actually tell us anything useful? Surely all it offers is some fairly obvious statements such as, for example, big, muscular hearty people are big, muscular and hearty. Even if that is true, it is hardly illuminating. Personality assessment, to be of any value, must be able to predict with some accuracy what a person will do in a variety of situations. The body type theory does not do that. For example, will the viscerotonic endomorph be aesthetically sensitive? Tense? Socially bold? Self-doubting? The theory is simply too simplistic to answer any of these questions. It is interesting as a curiosity, but for serious purposes it has no use.

The next major milestone in personality theory was laid by Jung. He had been a follower and close colleague of Freud's. Although they eventually fell out over theoretical differences, he advocated a theory that was much influenced by Freudian concepts. Jung talked of a psyche, which was made up of the ego and the unconscious, which itself took two forms: personal and collective. These systems were separate but interacted with each other. The personal unconscious consists of repressed individual experiences and is a concept quite familiar to us today. The collective unconscious also still has its proponents but is much more controversial. Jung held that the whole of humanity has access to a common unconscious and that this explains why all people react in a broadly similar way.

It was Jung who divided humanity into extroverts and introverts. Extroverts have an orientation toward the external, real world, while introverts prefer to look inward to their subjective experiences. People do not necessarily fall neatly into one category or the other, and even the most introverted among us have times when they are focused outwards. However, in the conscious mind one of these orientations will predominate. These basic orientations operate in conjunction with four functions that exist in all individuals. It is the interaction of orientation and function that forms the basis of personality. The four functions are:

SENSING: the reality function which gives factual representations of the world.

INTUITION: an unconscious process that looks beyond the surface of the 'real' world in the search for underlying factors that help an individual to comprehend the essence of reality.

THINKING: the rational observation of the world in terms of fact, logic and argument.

FEELING: an evaluative observation of self and the world in terms of emotions.

Sensing versus intuition, and thinking versus feeling are known as the two functions. One of the preferred functions is the dominant function and the other is the auxiliary. Thus an individual who is more sensing than intuiting and more thinking than feeling might have sensing as his dominant function and thinking as his auxiliary type. For another person who is also a sensing and thinking type, thinking might be the dominant function and sensing the auxiliary. The dominant function is used in the preferred attitude (extroversion or introversion). Introverts use their dominant function in the inner world; extroverts use their dominant function in the outer world. Conversely, the auxiliary function is used in the non-preferred attitude.

To determine a person's dominant and auxiliary function, Myers and Briggs derived an additional scale, judgement versus perception, in which a four-letter code can be used to indicate the individual's type. The judgement/perception (J-P) preference indicates the function that an individual uses when dealing with the outer world. Thus if judgement is preferred, either feeling or thinking (whichever is preferred) is used most in the outer world. If perception is preferred, either sensing or intuition (whichever is preferred) is used most in the outside world. The dominant function varies for extroverts and introverts. For extroverts the function to which J-P points is the dominant function and the other is the auxiliary. For introverts the reverse is the case. This Jungian typology, despite its age, is still very widely used in personality analysis.

Long after Jung, another psychologist, Hans Eysenck, produced a different typology, which has also received much attention (summarized in the diagram opposite).

Eysenck's work is a good illustration of trait theory in action. A trait is simply a description of a habitual behavior pattern.

Our language contains literally thousands of words that describe such patterns. These range from 'sociability' and 'persistence' to 'anxiety' and 'instability'. Many psychologists have tried to construct questionnaires to identify which of these traits describe a particular respondent. These seek to elicit information about the respondent's preferences, opinions and attitudes, the most common type being one that makes a series of statements with which the respondent is invited to agree or disagree. As there may be occasions on which no hard-and-fast answer can be given, there is usually a third option for those who wish to remain 'undecided'. In some tests the responses are more finely graded and will allow the respondent to answer on a five-point scale that goes from 1 (strongly agree) to 5 (strongly disagree), with 3 representing the point at which no firm decision can be made. The important feature of such questionnaires is that they do not have right or wrong answers. A statement such as 'I like going to parties' can elicit a 'yes' or 'no' response without the respondent feeling anxious that they have 'got it wrong'. Of course, there are circumstances in which respondents try to create an artificial impression of themselves but we will come to that later.

The history of psychometric personality

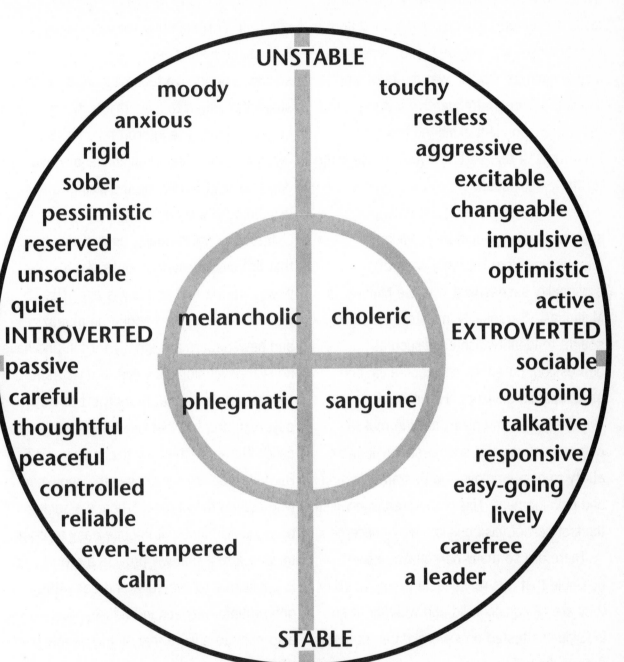

UNSTABLE

moody   touchy
anxious   restless
rigid   aggressive
sober   excitable
pessimistic   changeable
reserved   impulsive
unsociable   optimistic
quiet   active

melancholic   choleric

INTROVERTED   **EXTROVERTED**

phlegmatic   sanguine

passive   sociable
careful   outgoing
thoughtful   talkative
peaceful   responsive
controlled   easy-going
reliable   lively
even-tempered   carefree
calm   a leader

STABLE

EYSENCK'S TYPOLOGY

assessment began during the First World War when the American army was keen to ascertain whether recruits were emotionally disturbed before sending them into action. A questionnaire was devised, and investigated issues such as 'Do you wet the bed?' and 'Do you daydream frequently?' If it seemed that the respondent exhibited too many symptoms of this sort, he would be sent for further examination.

At first it seemed that the main use of such techniques would be medical. A famous test from the early days of personality assessment was the Minnesota Multiphasic Personality Inventory which sought to identify disorders such as depression, paranoia, schizophrenia, and psychopathic deviance. However, it eventually became clear that the real commercial value of such tests lay in their ability to help employers with staff selection and development. This is the area with which the first part of this book is mainly concerned.

There are so many personality tests available that it is reasonable to ask whether they are all equally valid and whether, if an individual is tested on several different tests, the results will be similar. The short answer is 'no'. It is true that those tests that rely on trait theory and that look at similar traits should produce broadly similar results. However, some tests are completely different. For example, the well-known Rorschach Inkblot Test is an example of a so-called projective technique in which the subject is asked to 'see' things in a series of colored blobs. The interpretation of the results of such tests is highly subjective and depends very largely on the skill of the psychologist involved.

It is also worth noting right at the start that not everything that looks like a psychometric test actually is one. The plethora of tests that appear in magazines and newspapers are strictly for fun and have no real psychological value. Rather more sinister are tests that do purport to be psychometric but that rely heavily on the so-called Barnum effect for their results. P.T. Barnum, you will recall, was the showman who coined the phrase, 'There's a sucker born every minute.' It is quite easy to come up with a test that will provide a report that is applicable to everyone and does not differentiate between individuals at all. It is also easy to ensure that all the people who receive a report from such a test will believe it to be an accurate picture of themselves.

the question of whether personality can be changed is vital to the whole area of personality assessment. Unfortunately, as with many questions in psychology, the answer is not straightforward. Part of the very definition of personality is (as we saw earlier) that it should be stable over time. You get up each morning the same person that went to bed last night. This is certainly our common experience of ourselves and the people we know, and we would be wary of someone who was subject to such violent personality changes that they seemed to become a different person within a short space of time. There are, indeed, examples of people with multiple personality disorder who *do* switch from one personality to another totally different one within a very short space of time. But we regard this as a psychiatric condition requiring medical intervention and not as in any way the norm. However, if people cannot change, then the benefits of personality assessment are much reduced. We can pick out people who might be suitable or unsuitable for particular situations. We can look at people working together and see who is likely to get on well and who is not. But if we cannot help people to change, then our role is a limited one.

The extent to which people are in control of their personality is controversial. Freud and Jung would have us believe that we are largely subject to the promptings of unconscious urges. This view has affected many areas of thought over the last century. In the arts, for example, it has been almost compulsory among academics to hold to the view that the artist is the last person to understand the work he or she has created. A novel, for example, is said to be full of the unconscious promptings of the author's psyche, and the author is ill-equipped to understand these promptings by virtue of the fact that, as they are unconscious, he or she is unaware of them.

Psychoanalysis is based on the principle that people will go on repeating a vicious circle of neurotic behavior until a qualified psychoanalyst helps them unravel the motives that drive them. This process is a very lengthy and expensive one and any change in behavior is only obtained after the most searching examination of the subject's childhood, formative experiences and relationships. A number of techniques, such as free association and dream analysis, are used in an attempt to get the patient to face the urges that have been hidden for so long. As much of the unconscious material consists of repressed memories of episodes in the patient's past that are too painful to be recalled, you may understand that the effort of uncovering such memories is very considerable.

At the other extreme we find the existentialist school, which teaches that we need not be bound by our past, and urges us to take personal responsibility for our lives. The message could not be more different. This is a passage from *Theory and Practice of Counselling and Psychotherapy* by Gerald Corey:

The existential view of human nature is captured, in part, by the notion that the significance of our existence is never fixed once and for all; rather, we continually recreate ourselves through our projects. Humans are in a constant state of transition, emerging, evolving, and becoming. Being a person implies that we are discovering and making sense of existence. We pose questions such as 'Who am I? Who have I been? Who can I become? Where am I going?' There are no pre-existing designs and no meanings that are assigned or given to us.

On a day-to-day basis we know that people do change. Usually the changes are small and happen over a long period, but they can be sudden and dramatic. Take, for example, someone who suffers the death of a partner. This may well result in a period of depression that could last months or even years, and in the long term we might notice a number of changes such as increased anxiety, a less extrovert orientation, even an increase in self-doubt and a decline in creativity. None of these changes would be set in stone, and if we were to imagine that our subject eventually meets a new partner, then we might see other more positive changes over time.

When we are testing people in an occupational setting we are continually aware of the possibility that changes in personality can be made. The particular report I use most has two sections at the end. The first is Potential Strengths, which, as you would expect, highlights positive areas that the subject should be encouraged to emphasize. The second section is Potential Development Needs, which, put plainly, is a list of things that are not an asset and that might benefit from change. One of the things we emphasize to clients is that your personality is not something fixed like, say, your shoe size, but something that, within certain limits, is capable of change. What those limits are is open to question. I should imagine that if an employee were to be called in for an appraisal interview after testing and was told, 'You could make management and get a pay rise if you could just learn to be a bit more friendly and outgoing with the customers,' the requirement might well be within that person's capability. Self-interest seems to be a powerful motivating factor in making such changes.

All changes in personality are likely to be stressful; therefore it makes sense to take things slowly. Start by working on aspects of your personality that you feel you could change without too much trouble. Remember that a dramatic change is unlikely to last.

What is almost certainly impossible and definitely ill-advised is the attempt to become a person you are quite clearly not. It is quite common to come across the sort of self-help books that promise the gullible reader the chance to acquire a new, more forceful, more dynamic personality. Naturally, the come-on at some point suggests that this 'new you' will also be more attractive to the opposite sex. Oh dear. The chance of such a bold enterprise ever succeeding must be almost incalculably small. It is not possible that a painfully shy person will overnight become

an outgoing one or that someone who is really rather passive will discover an as yet untapped vein of assertiveness. In any case, what is most attractive about a person is that part that is most natural and honest. People who give that up in order to make an impression usually look, to everyone except themselves, rather ridiculous.

This is never more clearly seen than in the media, when someone who starts out as an ordinary Joe with a bit of talent suddenly becomes a star. The transformation can be quite alarming and, for the person concerned, a complete disaster. How many such people have you seen start to believe their own publicity and become monsters of egotism? And how many of them then find themselves divorced from the people on whom they used to depend and completely at sea in a world that is utterly false? The numerous stories of pop stars, film stars, sports personalities and others who end up as victims of drink, drugs, depression and even violence are not coincidences. Losing your grip on your personality is a dangerous business.

One change that we all see taking place is the kind that affects people in long-term relationships. It can go either way. You often see couples who, having been together for years, have learned to accommodate each other by moving closer together in terms of

CAN YOU CHANGE?

personality. Alternatively, it is also quite common to come across people who have been driven apart by years of physical proximity and eventually become completely incompatible. This often leads to the tragic sight of a couple past middle-age and with their children having reached independence deciding to split up after years of barely concealed dislike.

As I mentioned earlier, we spend quite a bit of time constructing compatibility studies for people in relationships that seem to be in trouble. What is quite alarming is the degree to which people believe it is possible to keep their partner's 'good' bits and throw out the 'bad'. The problem is that not only do our tests ignore the sexual attraction in a relationship, they are also forced to leave out love. This is a significant omission but, to the best of my knowledge, there is no

reliable test for love on the market. Consequently I spend some of my time looking at relationships that, by all reasonable standards, are never going to work. The plain fact of the matter is that the people in these relationships do, despite my dispassionate analysis of their plight, dote on each other and are looking to me anxiously for some way in which to put the whole situation right. This is the sort of change that, I feel, is not going to be possible, and the quest for it is likely to cause considerable emotional pain to both the partners. We cannot love someone on condition that they become someone else. That seems obvious, but it is quite surprising how often people try to impose changes on each other in order to achieve a partner who is more 'acceptable'.

Conducting a psychometric test is of little benefit unless its results can be interpreted accurately and used to measure a person's individual abilities against the population as a whole, or at least the particular group of interest. Where the sample (the group of people participating in a test) increases in size, and different tests of varying levels of complexity are introduced, the raw results are rarely very informative. For instance, in terms of relative performance the 70% raw score, a 16-year-old achieves in his or her maths assessment cannot be compared to the 54% obtained by a graduate taking a professional accountancy examination. Which of the two performed better cannot be concluded just from this limited information. The performance of the base population, i.e. all 16-year-olds submitting this type of assessment, is consequently used to create a model against which individual scores can be placed to compare their achievements. This statistical model relies upon what is called the *Normal distribution*, which the 16-year-old's maths assessment will help explain.

Let's assume the maths assessment results varied from 40% to 95% and can be represented graphically as shown below:

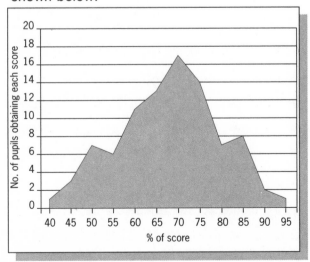

Out of the 90 pupils, 32 scored 75% or above. This shows that a score of 75% places a candidate at the lower end of the top 35% of pupils, or conversely at the top of the bottom 65%, in the 65th percentile. Clearly the assessment results vary in line with the number of students and the assessment itself. So such conclusions claiming the relative performance of a student with another become rather cumbersome when changes in the sample occur, with performances between different assessment groups being largely incomparable. This is where the Normal distribution offers some assistance.

If the assessment results are re-examined, we can see then that the average score is approximately 68%, found by summing all the scores and dividing by the number of pupils, 90. If the test results are redrawn around this mean, a curve can be fitted to represent an approximate scoring pattern:

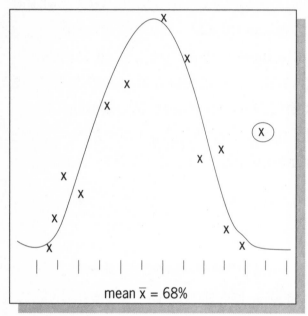

mean x̄ = 68%

This curve is known as the Normal distribution curve. It represents graphically the logical result that the largest proportion of a sample achieves the mean average score. The bell-shaped curve shows how, as the score increases or decreases from the mean of 68%, so too does the proportion of people achieving each score. As the sample size grows, the pattern of results fits the Normal curve more and more closely. This is because the population as a whole conforms to the Normal pattern. Therefore, as the sample size augments, it becomes better aligned to its parent population, and consequently provides a more accurate basis for comparison. With smaller samples, deviations from the Normal pattern are more likely to occur, i.e., an instance where 8 pupils miraculously score 95% in the assessment. Despite being positioned further away from the Normal curve, the distribution still holds, but its validity may be restricted. This will be explored in more depth later on.

So, as a basis for a model, the Normal distribution can be applied to events as diverse as psychometric testing and assessing the Australians' affinity for Earl Grey tea. However, certain characteristics intrinsic to the Normal curve render it a unique and an invaluable statistical tool. It always remains symmetrical about the mean, which is represented usually as the peak of the curve. This curve is approximately bell-shaped, and the area under it is equal to 100%, or 1. This 1 represents the whole population: if the peak point shows the average result, the scores up to that point are achieved by 50% of the pupils. Since the curve is symmetrical, 100% of the scores fall below the entire curve so all performances are accounted for. So just how does the Normal distribution provide a basis for comparison? A process of standardization is required to make results from a multitude of tests comparable.

This involves comparing the actual result with the average score in the context of a test situation, and incorporating a measure of spread, known as the Standard Deviation (SD). This provides a means of measuring numerically the extent to which scores deviate from the mean result. The two following samples emphasize the importance of this. The size of each sample is identical; it is the spread of results that varies.

The results of two psychometric tests have been plotted on the two graphs below, each following a Normal distribution. The 'Easy' sample is far more widely spread out about the mean than that of 'Peasy', which is more closely bunched. The mean = 50, and being the same for both groups, gives no indication of this spread. Enter the standard deviation.

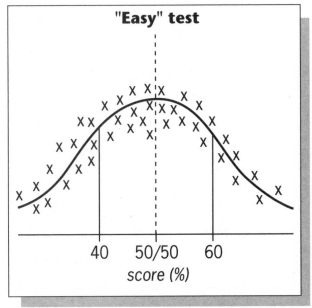

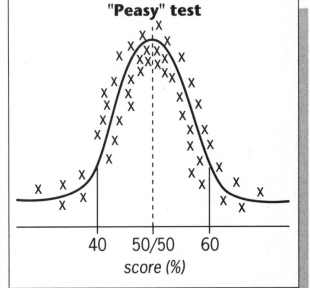

Due to the greater range of results in the 'Easy' test, a score of 40 is far more acceptable than the same grade in 'Peasy', as here far fewer people scored as low a grade. By applying standard deviations, it is possible to see the relative performance of each 40-scoring candidate. To activate their use, standard deviations are applied to the standardized scores, which enable the mean to be set equal to zero. This is important, as the multitude of means obtained from many different test samples can all be equated to 0 so a basis for comparison is established. The vast majority of a sample's results lie within three standard deviations of the mean. When this mean is equated to 0, this is depicted as shown below:

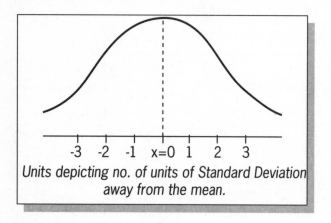

Units depicting no. of units of Standard Deviation away from the mean.

So at point 1, we are one standard deviation above the mean, and at −3, three standard deviations below.

As a rough guide:

68.3% of the population lie within 1 SD about the mean; 95.4% of the population lie within 2 SD about the mean; 99.7% of the population lie within 3 SD about the mean.

So the 'Easy' test would be expected to have a higher standard deviation value than 'Peasy' due to the greater range of results. Simplifying the results in graph form helps to clarify:

Test: no. of candidates obtaining score

Score(%)	Easy	Peasy
10	1	0
20	2	0
30	4	2
40	8	8
50	16	26
60	8	8
70	4	2
80	2	0
90	1	0

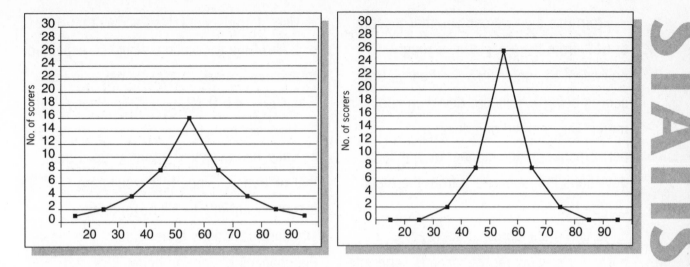

The Standard Deviation is found using the expression $SD = \sqrt{\dfrac{(X^2 - n\bar{x}^2}{n-1}}$
where x = each score, $\bar{x}$ = mean score, n = sample size, (= total sum

In other words, the standard deviation is found by summing the squared values of each score, subtracting the sample size multiplied by the mean value squared, dividing the answer by the sample size minus 1, and square-rooting the result. Applying this to the two samples yields:

Easy

$(x^2 = 1(10^2) + 2(20^2) + 4(30^2) + 8(40^2) + 16(50^2) + 8(60^2) + 4(70^2) + 2(80^2) + 1(90^2)$
= **126,600**

$\bar{x}$ = [(1(10) + 2(20) + 4(30 + 8(40) + 16(50) + 8(60) + 4(70) + 2(80) + 1(90)] 4 46
= **50**

$\bar{x}^2 = 50^2$ = **2500**

n − 1 = **45**

= . SD = $\sqrt{\dfrac{126,600 - (46 \times 2500)}{45}}$ = **16.1** *(to 1 decimal place)*

peasy

$(x^2 = 2(30^2) + 8(40^2) + 26(50^2) + 8(60^2) + 2(70^2)$ = **118,200**

$\bar{x}$ = [(2(30) + 8 (40) + 26 (50) + 8 (60) + 2 (70)] 4 46 = **50**

$\bar{x}^2 = 50^2$ = **2500**

n − 1 = **45**

= . SD = $\sqrt{\dfrac{118,200 - (46 \times 2500)}{45}}$ = **8.4** *(to 1 decimal place)*

From this then we can see that a score of 66% from the 'Easy' test is roughly equivalent to one of 58% for 'Peasy', both scores being 1 standard deviation above the mean. This method of judging a performance by the number of standard deviations that separate it from the mean can be helpful.

To find a standardized score, z, of a particular raw score, the mean is subtracted from the raw score, and this is then divided by the standard deviation. So for the two scores of 40%:

$$z\ easy = \frac{40 - 50}{16.1} = -0.6$$

$$z\ peasy = \frac{40 - 50}{8.4} = -1.2$$

Each score of 40 can thus be compared on the following standardized Normal curves:

Use of statistical tables shows that 0.27, or 27% of the population, would be expected to achieve a mark of 40% or below in the 'Easy' test and 0.12, or 12% in 'Peasy'.

Thus since $-0.6 > -1.2$, the scorer of 40 in 'Easy' has achieved a better result than that of 'Peasy'. Since test results are extremely unlikely to fall beyond three standard deviations either side of the mean, the chances of scoring below 25% and above 75% for the 'Peasy' test are virtually non-existent. This is less illuminating with the 'Easy' test: we conclude that results are likely to fall in the region 2%–98%, indicative of its far greater spread of results.

Importantly, the application of the Normal distribution is not restricted to groups of the same sample size. The 'Easy Peasy' examples take advantage of this fact to simplify the explanatory analysis. Rather, the Normal's merit lies in the fact that the test

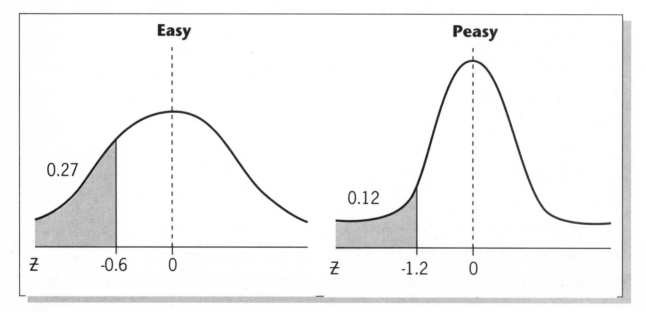

26

and standard deviation process can be applied to any set of test scores, regardless of test type, the scoring process and units used, and the mean and range of results.

Consequently, standard deviations are incorporated into the psychometric test-scoring process to help predict the proportion of people likely to achieve a test score lying between a specified number of standard deviations. For a psychometric test to be effective, it is essential to know the mean and standard deviation of the parent population either from existing data or from calculations using as large a relevant sample as possible. Using a relevant parent population or sample for this is absolutely vital in order for results to be accurately interpreted: standardizing the 16-year-olds' maths assessment mark by using the average mean mark for the same assessment obtained by a group of graduate statisticians is blatantly nonsensical. Due to this, for a particular test, various Normal tables may exist for different groups of people to allow reasonable comparisons to be made.

The use of the Normal distribution tables to assess psychometric test results is sometimes rejected in favor of converting the raw standardized **z** values to a scoring scale, the most popular of these being the stanine, sten and T-score scales. The same standardizing process is implemented; **z** scores are simply manipulated to form different bases for comparison.

All three scales are established by multiplying the **z** score by a certain factor, and adding this to their own particular mean. The sten and stanine scales both split their ranges up between two standard deviations about the mean, the former method being favoured by personality test assessment. In contrast, the T-score can span beyond three standard deviations. Computation is as follows:

Stanine $x = 2\bar{z} + 5$ $1 < x < 10$ $\bar{x} = 5$

Sten $x = 2\bar{z} + 5.5$ $1 < x < 9$ $\bar{x} = 5.5$

T-score $x = 10\bar{z} + 50$ $30 < x < 80$ $\bar{x} = 50$

RELIABILITY AND VALIDITY

Regardless of the length and complexity of a test, if it flounders in the reliability and validity stakes, it is of little use. A test has to be assessed in terms of both of these factors in order to ascertain how much it can be relied upon.

Should the same person take the same test on two consecutive occasions, the results should be very similar. The extent to which this consistency occurs is determined by the reliability level of a test, or the margin of error. Rather than questioning its accuracy, validity considers whether a test assesses what it claims to, e.g., does a numeracy test actually gauge numeracy or rather learning skills? The four main types of efficiency and validity that are of interest in the psychometric testing procedure are:

Test-retest *Determines a test's overall consistency*

Construct *Measures how well a test assesses what it claims to*

Internal consistency

Judges to what extent random groups of questions within a test assess the same thing

Criterion-related

Questions if a test can be practicably applied with objective, tangible results of same specified criterion, or if this criterion is too abstract and immeasurable

Clearly the nature of a psychometric test determines which strands of reliability and validity are of most concern. Since this varies with each situation (e.g., different tests may aim to boast high internal consistency rather than high criterion-related validity), combining a number of these contrasting tests helps to ensure that a balance of objectives is achieved.

Aside from the subjective appraisal of a test's reliability and validity, another statistical tool is on hand to quantify a test's performance in this domain: the correlation coefficient, **r**. This is used to measure the reliability and validity of tests by calculating the degree of association between two variables. A high correlation coefficient is obtained when both variables, or items of interest, are strongly related to each other 0 (see Figure **a** below). When one thing has little impact on the other's value, the correlation coefficient will be low (see Figure **b** on p.29). The following scattergrams exemplify both situations where each dot corresponds to an instance in which corresponding values on the horizontal and vertical axis simultaneously occur. Figure **a** demonstrates that the older

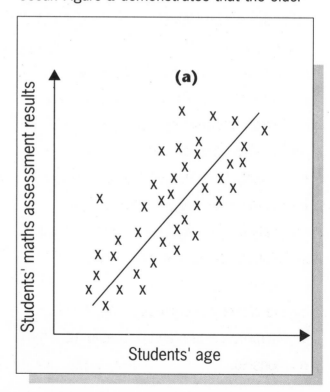

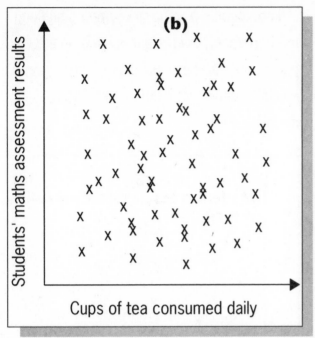

Students' maths assessment results

(b)

Cups of tea consumed daily

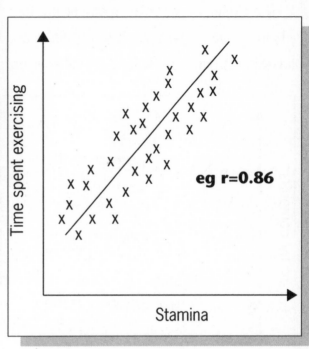

Time spent exercising

eg r=0.86

Stamina

the student, the higher the grade obtained in the standard maths assessment, as a rule. We can conclude that the correlation coefficient will be high. In contrast, the very low correlation between daily tea consumption and assessment performance shows how one variable cannot be used accurately to calculate the other; the two are unrelated. As the dots veer further away from the line representing the linear relationship between variables, as in (a), the relationship becomes weaker and harder to define. Consequently, the value of the correlation coefficient falls towards 0. The correlation can vary in value from -1 to 1:

r = 1

The closer the correlation coefficient to 1, the more perfect and definable the relationship.

r = 0

The closer the correlation coefficient to 0, the more negligible and less definable the relationship.

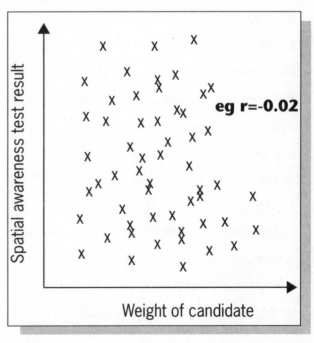

Spatial awareness test result

eg r=-0.02

Weight of candidate

r = –1

The closer the correlation coefficient to –1, the more perfect but negative the relationship: as one variable falls, the other rises.

In a specific psychometric test situation, the correlation coefficient is used as a guide, and can be applied to the four key reliability and validity concerns already mentioned:

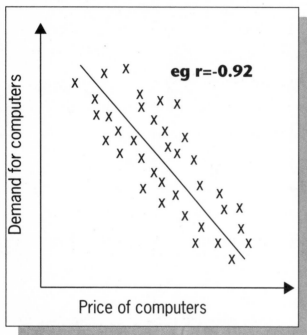

The correlation coefficient will rarely identify a perfect relationship because numerous other factors are often involved: the higher the price of computers, the lower the demand, but demand may also be affected by advertising, availability, computer performance and the state of the economy. So when using the correlation coefficient to assess the reliability and validity of psychometric tests, it is essential to consider the other factors involved. The correlation coefficient is used to aid the analysis, not to act as its sole determinant.

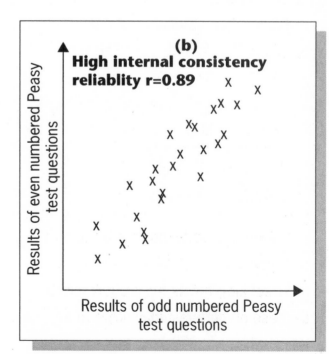

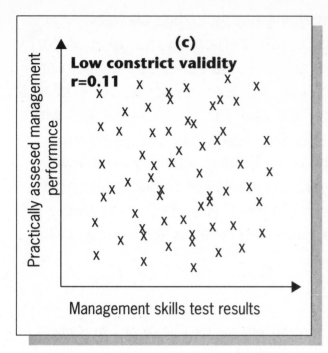

(c)
Low constrict validity
r=0.11

Practically assesed management performnce

Management skills test results

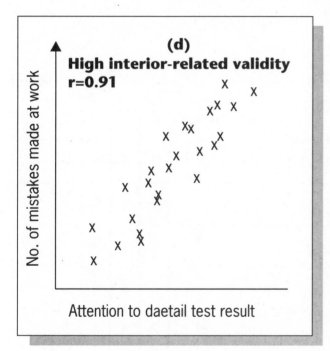

(d)
High interior-related validity
r=0.91

No. of mistakes made at work

Attention to daetail test result

Validity is of particular interest when considering the likelihood of making incorrect judgements from test results. In the case of (c), a test may prove to be invalid when a low score in the

management skills test later proves to be a poor indication of the actual high practical management performance. The importance of these validity tests is, then, in determining what proportion of test results will reflect accurately a candidate's true abilities and potential. Finding the ratio of likely correct-to-incorrect decisions helps determine this. Consequently, **psychometric tests are rarely the sole means of selection, but are used in conjunction with a more personal, subjective approach.**

Being harder to determine than reliability, acceptable levels of validity vary in accordance with both the test and previous selection procedures. Despite some low levels of test validity, the recent rise in popularity of psychometric testing in the selection process stems from the frequently lower validity of alternative assessment methods on offer. Given that psychometric tests are predominantly used in an interview/selection process, their results can be far more illuminating than any 20-minute interrogation. Should the validity of a test be low, the interviewer should realize this and gear his or her questions to reveal the true validity of an individual's test result. If you already know and understand what your psychometric test is likely to indicate, you are better equipped to argue against any misleading shortcomings it may expose.

ocus of control is something psychologists are very interested in when they assess personality, but what on earth is it? It sounds a bit like one of those bones in the inner ear that you didn't know you had. However, as far as personality is concerned, locus plays a vital role. Put simply, it decides who is in the driving seat of your life. Your locus can be internal, external or somewhere between the two, but its position will dramatically affect both your personality and your relationships. To find out where your locus of control is and what this means, answer the questions below and then read the explanation at the end of the game.

mark each of the following statements on a scale of 1 to 5 where 1 = Strongly agree, 2 = Agree, 3 = Not sure, 4 = Disagree, and 5 = Strongly disagree.

score

1.	I am the captain of my ship.	1	2	③	4	5	3
2.	You can't fight City Hall.	1	②	3	4	5	2
3.	Government is there to solve our problems.	1	2	3	④	5	4
4.	I can achieve anything if I try hard enough.	1	②	3	4	5	4
5.	I seldom admit defeat.	1	2	3	④	5	2
6.	I do not believe in free will.	①	2	3	4	5	1
7.	Fate plays an important part in my life.	1	2	③	4	5	3
8.	I prefer to fight my own battles.	1	2	3	④	5	2
9.	Issues in the modern world are often too complex to understand fully.	1	2	3	④	5	4

10.	I sometimes feel unable to cope.	①	2	3	4	5	*1*
11.	At work I like to be told exactly what to do.	1	②	3	4	5	*2*
12.	I would like to conduct an orchestra.	1	②	3	4	5	*4*
13.	Astrology has a profound influence on our lives.	1	2	3	4	⑤	*5*
14.	I frequently pray over my problems.	1	2	3	4	⑤	*5*
15.	I like to be left to get on with things.	①	2	3	4	5	*5*
16.	I am confident about the course my life is taking.	1	2	③	4	5	*3*
17.	Destiny plays no part in my life.	1	2	③	4	5	*3*
18.	Taking orders irritates me.	1	2	③	4	5	*3*
19.	I defer to my elders and betters.	1	2	3	④	5	*4*
20.	If you want something done properly, you have to do it yourself.	1	2	③	4	5	*3*
21.	We often need help and advice from our superiors.	1	②	3	4	5	*2*
22.	I like to be part of an organization.	1	2	3	④	5	*4*
23.	I admire cats for their independence.	1	②	3	4	5	*4*
24.	I enjoy working independently.	1	②	3	4	5	*4*
25.	I like someone else to check my work before it's finished.	1	2	3	④	5	*4*

For questions 1, 4, 5, 8, 12, 15, 16, 17, 18, 20, 23, and 24, give yourself 5 points for answer 1 (strongly agree), down to 1 point for answer 5 (strongly disagree). For questions 2, 3, 6, 7, 9, 10, 11, 13, 14, 19, 21, 22, and 25, give yourself 1 point for answer 1 (strongly agree), up to 5 points for answer 5 (strongly disagree). Maximum score is 75.

ARE YOU IN CONTROL?

THE SCORES

People with an internal locus believe that they are in charge of their own lives, are frequently optimists, and believe that they can overcome any obstacles. They tend to put very little faith in outside influences or regulating bodies such as governments, or more nebulous concepts such as luck or fate. By contrast, people who feel their lives are controlled by outside forces and that they are powerless to influence events are said to have an external locus; this is associated with a pessimistic attitude to life. In our test, the higher your score, the more internalized your locus.

65–75:

This shows you have a strongly internal locus. You are certainly not lacking confidence in yourself! But beware, you may overestimate your ability to influence your circumstances.

45–64:

You're pretty sure that you can control your life but are realistic enough to know that some situations are beyond your control. Your optimism helps you overcome difficulties, and you're wise enough to know when to give up.

35–44:

You are inclined to think you have things under control but you have some serious doubts.

You are aware that there are times when you feel overcome by events. You are optimistic but easily dented by harsh reality.

25–34:

You seriously doubt your ability to handle events and suspect that much of your life is beyond your control. Any optimistic feelings you have are very fragile indeed, and you are uncomfortably aware that you often fail.

15–24:

You have a rather pessimistic outlook and feel that most of the time you are controlled by events rather than vice versa. You would like to be more in control but have little confidence that you could bring it off.

5–14:

Your lack of confidence in your ability is a serious obstacle to you. It would certainly be worth trying to cultivate a more positive, confident attitude in order to exercise control over many events in your life.

Below 5:

Your locus of control is almost entirely external. This is a situation that requires some form of help. Your lack of confidence in your ability is so pronounced that it is adversely affecting your whole life. You really do need to be helped to see that you are not as powerless as you believe yourself to be.

oyalty is always prized as a great virtue but, sadly, is often hard to find. How often have you discovered that people will not do for you what you would be willing to do for them? Are you the sort of person who sticks by your friends no matter what, or would you rather assess each situation as it comes and decide what is the best move for you? This test is designed to find out just how loyal you are prepared to be.

1. You have arranged to meet an old friend, but a good business opportunity comes up unexpectedly on the same day. Do you:

			score
a.	Phone your friend and explain why you can't make it.	✓	2
b.	Try to rearrange the business appointment.		
c.	Get your secretary to phone your friend and make an excuse.		

2. You're talking with a group of people you really like when, to your surprise, they start to criticize one of your friends. Do you:

			score
a.	Come loudly to your friend's defence.		
b.	Say nothing but decide to ignore their criticisms.	✓	2
c.	Decide that your friend may have faults you had not recognized.		

3. Do you always vote for the same political party?

a. Usually.   **b.** I like to be free to change.   **c.** Always.   **score** ☐ 1

4. Do you prefer dogs to cats?

a. Yes.   **b.** No.   **c.** Not sure.   **score**

35

5. Would you continue to shop at a local store if a supermarket opened up down the road?

			score
a.	I'd go where things were cheapest.	✓	1
b.	I'd still go to the local store sometimes		
c.	I'd stay with my local store.		

6. You are in the army and have been sent to fight in a war of which you disapprove. Do you:

			score
a.	Desert.		
b.	Express your disapproval but continue to do your duty.	✓	2
c.	Get on with the job despite your private misgivings.		

7. You have been married for years, but have now fallen in love with a younger person. Do you:

			score
a.	Have a brief fling that you keep secret from your partner.		
b.	Leave your partner for the new person in your life.	✓	1
c.	Give up this affair and stay with your partner.		

8. You have been in the same job for 20 years when a new opportunity suddenly comes your way. Do you:

			score
a.	Grab the new job with alacrity.		
b.	Weigh up all the pros and cons before coming to a rational decision.	✓	2
c.	Decide you can't possibly leave your old firm, friends and colleagues.		

9. Your beloved dog falls ill. The vet's bills are terrific. Do you:

			score
a.	Pay up, even though it hurts you financially.	✓	3
b.	Have the dog put down.		
c.	Get the vet to give you a cool assessment of the dog's chances before making a decision.		

10. Your best friend is found guilty of a serious crime. Do you:

			score
a.	Accept the court's verdict and break off contact with your friend.	✓	2
b.	Accept that your friend is guilty but try to offer support for old time's sake.		
c.	Refuse to acknowledge the verdict and battle for your friend's release.		

11. Do you support a regular sports team regardless of their results?

			score
a.	I'd never change my team.		
b.	I don't support anyone in particular.	✓	1
c.	I sometimes change allegiance.		

12. Do you believe in the saying, 'My country right or wrong'?

a. No.   **b.** To some extent.   **c.** Yes.   **score** ☐ 2

13. Do you believe that blood is thicker than water?

a. Yes.   **b.** No.   **c.** Not sure.   **score** ☐ 2

14. You win a lot of money in a lottery. Do you:

			score
a.	Detach yourself from your old friends because they cannot share your new world.		
b.	Try to keep in touch with people you used to know.		
c.	Make sure your friends continue to surround you, and share your good fortune with them.	✓	3

15. You discover that your partner has been having an affair. Do you:

			score
a.	Throw him/her out.	✓	1
b.	Insist on a trial separation to see if you still care for each other.		
c.	Do everything you can to hold on to the one you love.		

16. Do you ever go to old school or work reunions?

a. Frequently. **b.** Never. **c.** Sometimes. **score** 2

17. Do you always buy the same daily newspaper.

a. No. **b.** Usually. **c.** Yes. **score** 1

18. Do you have many friends who have known you for most of your life?

a. No. **b.** Yes. **c.** A few. **score** 2

19. Do you keep in touch with distant relations even though you do not much enjoy their company?

		score
a.	I make a point of it..	
b.	I try not to see them more than I have to.	✓ 1
c.	I contact them when I can.	

20. A long-term employee of your company is caught pilfering office stationery. Do you:

		score
a.	Fire him immediately.	
b.	Give him another chance.	
c.	Give him a trial period before making a decision.	✓ 2

21. You go regularly to the same restaurant. One day you get a bad meal there. Do you:

		score
a.	Complain but give them another chance.	
b.	Decide to change restaurants.	
c.	Carry on going.	✓ 3

22. How highly do you rate loyalty in your list of desirable characteristics?

		score
a.	Very highly.	
b.	Quite highly.	
c.	There are many more important things.	✓ 1

23. A friend is accused of a crime. You have no idea whether or not he is guilty. Would you lie to give him an alibi?

a. Absolutely not.   **b.** Perhaps.   **c.** Of course.   **score** ☐

24. Would you die for the sake of your friends?

a. Perhaps.   **b.** Certainly.   **c.** Probably not.   **score** ☐

25. A friend does something that harms you. Would you:

		score
a.	End the friendship.	
b.	Try to find out the reasons before acting.	✓ 2
c.	Feel hurt but continue the friendship anyway.	

SCORING KEY

For each answer score the number of points indicated.

1. a:2, b:3, c:1	**8.** a:1, b:2, c:3	**15.** a:1, b:2, c:3	**22.** a:3, b:2, c:1
2. a:3, b:2, c:1	**9.** a:3, b:1, c:2	**16.** a:3, b:1, c:2	**23.** a:1, b:2, c:3
3. a:2, b:1, c:3	**10.** a:1, b:2, c:3	**17.** a:1, b:2, c:3	**24.** a:2, b:3, c:1
4. a:3, b:1, c:2	**11.** a:3, b:1, c:2	**18.** a:1, b:3, c:2	**25.** a:1, b:2, c:3
5. a:1, b:2, c:3	**12.** a:1, b:2, c:3	**19.** a:3, b:1, c:2	
6. a:1, b:2, c:3	**13.** a:3, b:1, c:2	**20.** a:1, b:3, c:2	
7. a:2, b:1, c:3	**14.** a:1, b:2, c:3	**21.** a:2, b:1, c:3	

Over 65

Maximum score is 75. If you scored 65 or above, you are ferociously loyal. There is nothing you would not do or dare for those you consider to be your friends. You even continue this loyalty when it is not deserved or reciprocated.

50–64

If you scored 50 to 64, you are very loyal and generally give your friends the benefit of the doubt, but you are not so blinded by loyalty that you cannot see faults.

40–49

If you scored 40 to 49. you are capable of being loyal but also have a streak of self-interest that makes you think twice before supporting a friend in difficulty.

20–39

If you scored 20 to 39, you are mainly interested in yourself and give very little thought to the needs of those who might have a claim to your loyalty.

Below 20

If you scored below 20, you probably have no idea what this test is about.

do you greet each new day with a spring in your step and a song in your heart? Or is your life rather grey and lacking in sparkle? Happiness is one of the most important factors in mental health but it is hard to decide what gives rise to it. There are all sorts of material considerations like income, family relationships, contentment at work and so on that are clearly involved in how happy we are, but that is seldom the whole story. Some people have a sunny disposition despite their difficulties, while others manage to be miserable in spite of living in great comfort. Find out how you measure up by answering the following questions.

1. Do you wake up looking forward to a new day?

a. Always.   **b.** Sometimes.   **c.** Rarely.

score ☐ 2

2. Do you enjoy your work?

a. Not much. **b.** A bit.   **c.** Very much.

score ☐ 2

3. Do you have many friends?

a. Lots.   **b.** A reasonable number.

c. Not many.   score ☐ 2

4. Are you in a stable relationship?

a. No.   **b.** Yes. **c.** Not at the moment.

score ☐ 3

5. Does the state of the world concern you?

a. Sometimes.   **b.** Yes.   **c.** No.

score ☐ 2

6. Do you feel confident about your future?

a. No. **b.** Yes. **c.** In between.   score ☐ 3

7. Do you worry about political issues?

a. Never.   **b.** Sometimes.   **c.** Frequently.

score ☐ 3

8. Are you financially secure?

a. In between. **b.** Yes. **c.** No.   score ☐ 2

9. Do you have interests apart from your work?

a. Many. **b.** Some.   **c.** Few.   score ☐ 2

10. Do you bear your troubles cheerfully?

a. No. **b.** Unsure.   **c.** Yes.   score ☐ 3

11. Do you suffer from fits of anxiety?

a. Sometimes.   **b.** Often.   **c.** Rarely.

score ☐ 2

41

12. Do you have a religious faith of any sort?
a. Yes.   **b.** Unsure.   **c.** No.   **score** `1`

13. Do you feel that the world is a safe place to bring children into?
a. No.   **b.** Yes.   **c.** Unsure.   **score** `3`

14. Do you often feel lonely?
a. Often.   **b.** Sometimes.   **c.** Seldom.   **score** `2`

15. Would you like to change lives with someone else?
a. Certainly.   **b.** Perhaps.   **c.** No.   **score** `3`

16. Is your family life happy?
a. Usually.   **b.** Seldom.   **c.** Sometimes.   **score** `2`

17. Do you worry about old age?
a. Often.   **b.** Sometimes.   **c.** Seldom.   **score** `3`

18. Could you be poor but happy?
a. Unsure.   **b.** No.   **c.** Yes.   **score** `3`

19. Do you enjoy making plans for the future?
a. Often.   **b.** Seldom.   **c.** Sometimes.   **score** `3`

20. Do you bounce back from misfortune?
a. Easily.   **b.** Reasonably well.
c. With difficulty.   **score** `2`

21. Do you regard yourself as a happy person?
a. Usually.   **b.** Seldom.   **c.** Sometimes.   **score** `2`

22. Would you like to change your job?
a. Yes.   **b.** Unsure.   **c.** No.   **score** `2`

23. Do you have many regrets about the way your life has gone?
a. Some.   **b.** Few.   **c.** Many.   **score** `3`

24. Do you sleep well?
a. Usually.   **b.** Sometimes.   **c.** Seldom.   **score** `3`

25. Do you generally enjoy good health?
a. No.   **b.** In between.   **c.** Yes.   **score** `2`

SCORING KEY

For each answer score the number of points indicated.

1. a:3, b:2, c:1	**8.** a:2, b:3, c:1	**15.** a:1, b:2, c:3	**22.** a:1, b:2, c:3
2. a:1, b:2, c:3	**9.** a:3, b:2, c:1	**16.** a:3, b:1, c:2	**23.** a:2, b:3, c:1
3. a:3, b:2, c:1	**10.** a:1, b:2, c:3	**17.** a:1, b:2, c:3	**24.** a:3, b:2, c:1
4. a:1, b:3, c:2	**11.** a:2, b:1, c:3	**18.** a:2, b:1, c:3	**25.** a:1, b:2, c:3
5. a:2, b:1, c:3	**12.** a:3, b:2, c:1	**19.** a:3, b:1, c:2	
6. a:1, b:3, c:2	**13.** a:1, b:3, c:2	**20.** a:3, b:2, c:1	
7. a:3, b:2, c:1	**14.** a:1, b:2, c:3	**21.** a:3, b:1, c:2	

Over 65

Maximum score is 75. If you scored over 65, you really seem to have little to worry about. You are one of those people for whom life is just a sunny day, and the rest of us can but envy you.

55–64

If you scored between 55 and 64, you are still pretty satisfied with life, and there are very few clouds in your sky. You have occasional worries, but by and large you know how to deal with them.

45–54

With a score of between 45 and 54, you are capable of enjoying happiness, but your life has a few rocky patches that make it hard for you to be as happy as you would like.

35–44

If you scored between 35 and 44, you are really quite beset by troubles and seem to have difficulty in finding real happiness.

24–34

A score from 25 to 34 indicates that you have real problems and don't find much joy in your life at all. At this level of unhappiness you might well consider some sort of counselling to help you.

Below 25

If you scored below 25, then you really are suffering. Your life seems bleak and joyless in the extreme, and you would do well to seek professional help.

S ome people find themselves permanently at odds with life. They feel unwell for no good reason, unlucky, unloved and unappreciated. This is what is called emotional instability. Others are quite confident about their lives and are happy, healthy and feel themselves loved. This test will indicate just how emotionally stable you are.

1. Do you blush often?

a. Yes. **b.** No. **c.** Occasionally. **score** ☐ 1

2. Do you suffer from tension headaches?

a. Yes. **b.** No. **c.** Sometimes. **score** ☐ 2

3. Do you worry about your health?

a. Often. **b.** Sometimes. **c.** Never.

score ☐ 2

4. Do you feel that your life is meaningless?

a. Sometimes. **b.** Never. **c.** Often.

score ☐ 1

5. Do you worry a lot about little things?

a. No. **b.** Yes. **c.** Sometimes.

score ☐ 2

6. Do you sometimes feel that you get blamed unfairly?

a. Yes. **b.** Perhaps. **c.** No.

score ☐ 1

7. Do you feel that most people are luckier than you?

a. Definitely. **b.** Possibly. **c.** Not really.

score ☐ 1

8. Do you suffer from fits of remorse?

a. Sometimes. **b.** Often. **c.** Never.

score ☐ 2

9. Are you worried by untidy surroundings?

a. No. **b.** A bit. **c.** Yes. **score** ☐ 3

10. Do you smile and laugh often?

a. Quite often. **b.** Very often. **c.** Seldom

score ☐ 2

11. Do you consider yourself a happy person?

a. Not very. **b.** Moderately. **c.** Quite happy.

score ☐ 2

12. Is your life fulfilling?

a. No. **b.** Yes. **c.** Not bad. **score** ☐ 3

13. Do you make satisfactory relationships?

a. No. **b.** Yes. **c.** Sometimes.

score [1]

14. Do you have many friends?

a. Yes. **b.** Not that many. **c.** No.

score [2]

15. Were your parents happily married?

a. Unsure. **b.** Yes. **c.** No. score [1]

16. Do you wish you were somebody else?

a. Often. **b.** Never. **c.** Occasionally.

score [1]

17. Are you satisfied with your appearance?

a. Reasonably. **b.** No. **c.** Yes.

score [2]

18. Do you feel that other people respect you sufficiently?

a. No. **b.** Yes. **c.** Unsure.

score [1]

19. Do you often feel listless for no good reason?

a. Sometimes. **b.** Never. **c.** Often.

score [2]

20. Do you think the future holds good things for you?

a. I hope so. **b.** I doubt it. **c.** I'm sure it does.

score [1]

21. Have you ever thought that life is not worth the effort?

a. Yes. **b.** No. **c.** Sometimes.

score [2]

22. Do you suffer from morbid fears?

a. Not really. **b.** Yes. **c.** Occasionally.

score [1]

23. Do people take to you readily?

a. Mostly. **b.** Seldom. **c.** Sometimes.

score [ ]

24. Do you enjoy your job?

a. Yes. **b.** No. **c.** Unsure. score [2]

25. Would you change your life if you could?

a. Certainly. **b.** Probably. **c.** No.

score [2]

ARE YOU STABLE?

SCORING KEY

For each answer score the number of points indicated.

1. a:3, b:1, c:2	**8.** a:2, b:3, c:1	**15.** a:2, b:1, c:3	**22.** a:1, b:3, c:2
2. a:3, b:1, c:2	**9.** a:1, b:2, c:3	**16.** a:3, b:1, c:2	**23.** a:1, b:3, c:2
3. a:3, b:2, c:1	**10.** a:2, b:1, c:3	**17.** a:2, b:3, c:1	**24.** a:1 , b:3, c:2
4. a:2, b:1, c:3	**11.** a:3, b:2, c:1	**18.** a:3, b:1, c:2	**25.** a:3, b:2, c:1
5. a:1, b:3, c:2	**12.** a:3, b:1, c:2	**19.** a:2, b:1, c:3	
6. a:3, b:2, c:1	**13.** a:3, b:1, c:2	**20.** a:2, b:3, c:1	
7. a:3, b:2, c:1	**14.** a:1, b:2, c:3	**21.** a:3, b:1, c:2	

Over 70

Maximum score is 75. If you scored over 70, you are showing signs of being deeply unhappy with your life. As these tests are not in any way scientific, it would be silly to base an important decision on the outcome, but since you seem so deeply depressed, you might consider some form of therapy.

55–69

A score of 55 to 69 indicates quite a high degree of instability and might indicate that you really feel at odds with what is going on in your life. Some serious consideration of your problems is indicated.

45–54

A score of 45 to 54 is reasonable but still shows that you have areas of your life where you are quite deeply unhappy. You might benefit from some help dealing with your problems.

35–44

A score of 35 to 44 denotes a stable and well-adjusted individual. You have your worries but, by and large, you know how to take care of them.

20–34

A score of 20 to 34 indicates someone who is really very stable and has life well under control.

Below 20

A score below 20 is to be deeply envied. Nothing at all takes the shine off your life and the rest of us can only stand by in helpless admiration.

S ome people are noted for saying what they mean and meaning what they say. However, such people, though admirable, can be a little hard to live with. The unvarnished truth is often not quite what you want to hear. On the other hand many people indulge in what psychologists call 'self-monitoring behavior'. These are the people who think a little before they speak, weigh up the effect their words might have on others and, if necessary, alter what they were going to say to something a little less controversial. They would think of this behavior as tactful and diplomatic; others would describe it as disingenuous or even sneaky. Try the following test and see if you are adept at self-monitoring.

1. Can you laugh convincingly at other people's jokes even if you don't find them funny?
a. No. **b.** Yes. **c.** Perhaps.   **score** [3]

2. Would you start a political discussion with someone you didn't know well?
a. Yes. **b.** No. **c.** Unsure.   **score** [2]

3. If you were discussing religion with someone whose views you did not share, would you:
a. Express your own views forcibly.
b. Try to find a compromise.
c. Give the other person the impression that you agreed with them without actually saying so.
   score [2]

4. When political canvassers call at your door, do you express your real views to them?
a. Always.   **b.** Sometimes.   **c.** Never.
   score [ ]

5. Do you consider it more important to be truthful than to be tactful?
a. No.   **b.** Yes. **c.** Not sure. **score** [1]

6. Could you be successful as a second-hand car salesperson?
a. Unsure. **b.** Yes.   **c.** No.   **score** [2]

7. Would you make a good politician?
a. No. **b.** Yes. **c.** Unsure.   **score** [1]

8. Do you agree with the statement, 'Everyone tells white lies now and again'?
a. Yes. **b.** No. **c.** Unsure. **score** `3`

9. Have you ever complimented someone on their appearance without really meaning it?
a. No. **b.** Yes. **c.** Unsure. **score** `3`

10. Do you listen politely to people with whom you deeply disagree?
a. Yes. **b.** No. **c.** Unsure. **score** `3`

11. Do you consider what answer someone expects of you before making a reply?
a. Unsure. **b.** No. **c.** Yes. **score** `3`

12. Would you like to be a lawyer?
a. Yes. **b.** Unsure. **c.** No. **score** `1`

13. Do you expect people to take you at your word?
a. Always. **b.** Seldom. **c.** Sometimes. **score** `2`

14. Do you value your reputation for straight talking?
a. Very much. **b.** Not really. **c.** Not sure. **score** `3`

15. Would you express your opinions even at the risk of being unpopular?
a. Yes. **b.** No. **c.** Perhaps. **score** `1`

16. Do you find it hard to know what your true opinion is?
a. No. **b.** Sometimes. **c.** Yes. **score** `2`

17. Is it important to you that people trust your word without question?
a. Unsure. **b.** Yes **c.** No. **score** `-3`

18. Could you easily argue a case for and against the same proposition?
a. Yes. **b.** No. **c.** Unsure. **score** `2`

19. Do you have the gift of the gab?
a. Unsure. **b.** No. **c.** Yes. **score** `1`

20. Could you sell something you knew to be faulty?
a. Yes. **b.** No. **c.** Unsure. **score** `1`

21. Do you try to appear agreeable even to people you dislike?
a. Sometimes. **b.** Seldom. **c.** Often. **score** `3`

22. Would you keep the peace by telling people what they wanted to hear?
a. Yes. **b.** No. **c.** Maybe. **score** `3`

23. If you served on a jury, would you be prepared to stand alone against the decision of your colleagues?
a. Yes. **b.** Unsure. **c.** No. **score** `1`

24. Do you think of yourself as tactful and diplomatic?

a. Unsure. **b.** Yes. **c.** No. **score** 3

25. Do you think of yourself as outspoken and principled?

a. Yes. **b.** No. **c.** Unsure. **score** 3

SCORING KEY

For each answer score the number of points indicated.

1. a:1, b:3, c:2	**8.** a:3, b:1, c:2	**15.** a:1, b:3, c:2	**22.** a:3, b:1, c:2
2. a:1, b:3, c:2	**9.** a:1, b:3, c:2	**16.** a:1, b:2, c:3	**23.** a:1, b:2, c:3
3. a:1, b:2, c:3	**10.** a:3, b:1, c:2	**17.** a:2, b:1, c:3	**24.** a:2, b:3, c:1
4. a:1, b:2, c:3	**11.** a:2, b:1, c:3	**18.** a:3, b:1, c:2	**25.** a:1, b:3, c:2
5. a:3, b:1, c:2	**12.** a:3, b:2, c:1	**19.** a:2, b:1, c:3	
6. a:2, b:3, c:1	**13.** a:1, b:3, c:2	**20.** a:3, b:1, c:2	
7. a:1, b:3, c:2	**14.** a:1, b:3, c:2	**21.** a:2, b:1, c:3	

Over 60

Maximum score 75. If you scored over 60, you are very concerned to conceal your true feelings from others. You do not lie from malice, but you are unwilling to suffer the inconvenience of honest debate.

60–69

This range indicates that you are still very concerned not to cause offence, but might occasionally state an unwelcome truths.

50–59

This score suggests that you would rather be kind than truthful, but you are also capable of dealing with people honestly.

30–49

You tend to be quite honest, and will say what you mean. However, you are aware that some opinions may be hurtfuly, and will soften your words to avoid trouble.

20–29

This score indicates that you are quite outspoken and do not care much whether people like what you say or not.

Below 20

This score indicates that you are very honest but have no tact at all. People will respect the fact that you tell the truth as you see it, but they may not like your bluntness.

do you prefer thought to action? People are often divided into 'thinkers' and 'doers'. The two groups are usually not very impressed with each other. The doers see themselves as practical, level-headed and sensible. They refer to the thinkers as daydreamers who may be well-intentioned but are quite useless at getting things done. The thinkers, of course, do not share this view. They see themselves as intelligent, serious-minded and reflective, and they view the doers as brash, shallow and immature. Try the following questions and see where you fit in.

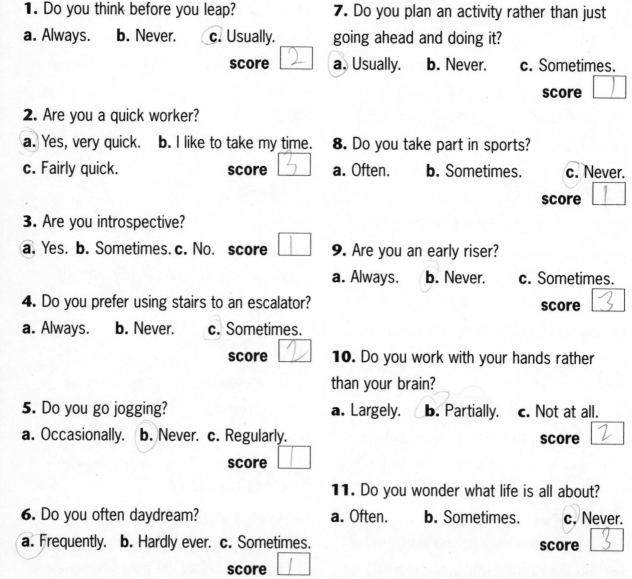

1. Do you think before you leap?

a. Always.   **b.** Never.   **c.** Usually.

score [2]

2. Are you a quick worker?

a. Yes, very quick.   **b.** I like to take my time.

c. Fairly quick.   **score** [3]

3. Are you introspective?

a. Yes. **b.** Sometimes. **c.** No.   **score** [1]

4. Do you prefer using stairs to an escalator?

a. Always.   **b.** Never.   **c.** Sometimes.

score [2]

5. Do you go jogging?

a. Occasionally.   **b.** Never.   **c.** Regularly.

score [ ]

6. Do you often daydream?

a. Frequently.   **b.** Hardly ever.   **c.** Sometimes.

score [1]

7. Do you plan an activity rather than just going ahead and doing it?

a. Usually.   **b.** Never.   **c.** Sometimes.

score [1]

8. Do you take part in sports?

a. Often.   **b.** Sometimes.   **c.** Never.

score [1]

9. Are you an early riser?

a. Always.   **b.** Never.   **c.** Sometimes.

score [3]

10. Do you work with your hands rather than your brain?

a. Largely.   **b.** Partially.   **c.** Not at all.

score [2]

11. Do you wonder what life is all about?

a. Often.   **b.** Sometimes.   **c.** Never.

score [3]

12. Do you rush about when busy?
a. Yes. **b.** Sometimes. **c.** No. **score** 3

13. Do you enjoy doing puzzles?
a. No. **b.** Occasionally. **c.** Yes. **score** 1

14. Are you a good talker?
a. Yes. **b.** No. **c.** Not bad. **score** 3

15. Would you enjoy abseiling?
a. No. **b.** Not sure. **c.** Yes. **score** 2

16. Do you prefer an activity holiday?
a. Yes. **b.** Sometimes. **c.** No. **score** 1

17. Would you like to belong to an amateur theatrical group?
a. No. **b.** Possibly. **c.** Yes. **score** 1

18. Are you a white-collar worker?
a. No. **b.** Not applicable. **c.** Yes. **score** 0

19. Are you good at mental arithmetic?
a. Yes. **b.** Not bad. **c.** No. **score** 1

20. Are you a fast reader?
a. Yes. **b.** Middling. **c.** No. **score** 2

21. Do you easily get depressed?
a. Yes. **b.** No. **c.** In between. **score** 1

22. Do you enjoying playing chess?
a. No. **b.** Sometimes. **c.** Yes. **score** 1

23. Do you like to gamble?
a. Sometimes. **b.** Yes. **c.** No. **score** 2

24. Are you early for appointments?
a. Always. **b.** Sometimes. **c.** Never. **score** 2

25. Do you believe that you could write a book?
a. Yes. **b.** Not sure. **c.** No. **score** 1

26. Would you rather go for a walk than sit and read a book?
a. Never. **b.** Sometimes. **c.** Usually. **score** 2

27. Could you build a shed?
a. No problem. **b.** Maybe. **c.** No way. **score** 3

28. Do you repair broken objects immediately?
a. Always. **b.** Sometimes. **c.** Never. **score** 2

29. Could you learn lines for a play?
a. No problem. **b.** Couldn't do it.
c. If I worked at it. **score** 2

30. Would you join a team of mountaineers?
a. Yes, I'd love to. **b.** I wouldn't dare.
c. I'd certainly consider it. **score** 1

31. Do you enjoy 'do-it-yourself' projects?
a. Yes. **b.** Sometimes. **c.** No. **score** 3

32. Do you like making speeches?
a. Yes. **b.** No. **c.** Don't mind. **score** 2

33. Do you like to exercise?
a. Often. **b.** Sometimes. **c.** Never.
score 1

34. Would you like to play bridge?
a. Yes. **b.** No. **c.** Uncertain. **score** 1

35. Would you ride on a roller-coaster?
a. Yes, with pleasure. **b.** No, I'd be terrified.
c. I wouldn't mind. **score** 1

36. Have you ever camped out all night?
a. Often. **b.** Never. **c.** Occasionally.
score 2

37. Did you excel at sport at school?
a. Yes. **b.** No. **c.** I did quite well.
score 1

38. Would you enjoy skiing?
a. Yes. **b.** No. **c.** Don't know. **score** 1

39. Do you have help with gardening?
a. No. **b.** Yes. **c.** Sometimes. **score** 3

40. Do you like poetry?
a. Yes. **b.** No. **c.** In between. **score** 1

41. Do you clean all your own window?
a. Yes. **b.** No. **c.** Sometimes. **score** 3

42. Do you like being outdoors a lot?
a. Yes. **b.** No. **c.** In between. **score** 2

43. Do you sleep more than eight hours?
a. Sometimes. **b.** Never. **c.** Always.
score 2

44. Have you ever wanted to own a sports car?
a. Yes, frequently. **b.** I've considered it.
c. Not my scene. **score** 1

45. Would you enjoy an evening spent
reading a good book?
a. Certainly. **b.** Possibly. **c.** Definitely not.
score 2

46. Would you volunteer for a moon trip?
a. Possibly. **b.** Certainly. **c.** Absolutely not.
score 1

47. Would you enjoy fishing?
a. Yes. **b.** No. **c.** Don't know. **score** 1

48. Do you wear smart clothes?
a. Sometimes. **b.** Always. **c.** Seldom.
score 2

49. Do you enjoy going to lectures?
a. Yes. **b.** No. **c.** Not sure. **score** 2

50. Do you hope that you will be very rich?
a. Yes. **b.** No. **c.** Don't think about it.
score 2

52

SCORING KEY

For each answer score the number of points indicated.

1. a:1, b:3, c:2	14. a:3, b:1, c:2	27. a:3, b:2, c:1	40. a:1, b:3, c:2
2. a:3, b:1, c:2	15. a:1, b:2, c:3	28. a:3, b:2, c:1	41. a:3, b:1, c:2
3. a:1, b:2, c:3	16. a:3, b:2, c:1	29. a:3, b:1, c:2	42. a:3, b:1, c:2
4. a:3, b:1, c:2	17. a:1, b:2, c:3	30. a:3, b:1, c:2	43. a:2, b:3, c:1
5. a:2, b:1, c:3	18. a:3, b:0, c:1	31. a:3, b:2, c:1	44. a:3, b:2, c:1
6. a:1, b:3, c:2	19. a:1, b:2, c:3	32. a:3, b:1, c:2	45. a:1, b:2, c:3
7. a:1, b:3, c:2	20. a:1, b:2, c:3	33. a:3, b:2, c:1	46. a:2, b:3, c:1
8. a:3, b:2, c:1	21. a:1, b:3, c:2	34. a:1, b:3, c:2	47. a:1, b:3, c:2
9. a:1, b:3, c:2	22. a:3, b:2, c:1	35. a:3, b:1, c:2	48. a:2, b:3, c:1
10. a:3, b:2, c:1	23. a:2, b:3, c:1	36. a:3, b:1, c:2	49. a:1, b:3, c:2
11. a:1, b:2, c:3	24. a:3, b:2, c:1	37. a:3, b:1, c:2	50. a:3, b:1, c:2
12. a:3, b:2, c:1	25. a:1, b:2, c:3	38. a:3, b:1, c:2	
13. a:3, b:2, c:1	26. a:1, b:2, c:3	39. a:3, b:1, c:2	

Over 125

The maximum score is 150. If you got over 125, quiet reflection holds no charms for you, and you would not know an introspective thought if it bit you. You are a great person for getting things done as long as someone else tells you what to do.

100–124

IThis range indicates that you are very active but not to the exclusion of all else. You are the sort of person who can be relied upon in a crisis, and you will also be able to consider the consequences of your actions.

50–99

A score of 50 to 99 suggests that you are much more at home in the realms of thought, but you are not hopelessly impractical and will be quite able to take action when you really have to.

Below 50

A score below 50 suggests that you don't really have much talent for action at all and are much more at home with a good book or an interesting idea. And why not? There's no shortage of people who want to rush around doing things, is there?

ntuition is a faculty that causes intense disagreement between those who believe strongly in it and those who don't. Jung regarded it as an important function of the human mind, and many thousands of people who 'feel' their way through life would agree with him. Opposed to them are those who think there is no substitute for hard facts and cold logic and that so-called intuition is just a lot of nonsense. Which type are you? The following questions should give you a pretty good idea of your orientation. Try to answer each question without hesitation. If you have to think before you answer, that in itself will tell you something about whether you are intuitive or logical!

1. Do you usually win at gambling?
Yes (B) ✳   No (A)   **score** ☐ 0

2. Do you trust your feelings even when they seem to be irrational?
Yes (B) ✳   No (A)   **score** ☐ 2

3. Do you like to look beneath the surface of human relationships?
Yes (B) ✳   No (A)   **score** ☐ 2

4. Have you ever used a ouija board?
Yes (B) ✳   No (A)   **score** ☐ 2

5. Are you superstitious?
Yes (B) ✳   No (A)   **score** ☐ 2

6. Do you feel that certain places have an 'atmosphere'?
Yes (B) ✳   No (A)   **score** ☐ 2

7. Do you usually win at guessing games?
Yes (B) ✳   No (A)   **score** ☐ 2

8. Do you sometimes distrust a person without reason?
Yes (B) ✳   No (A)   **score** ☐ 2

9. Would you attend a seance?
Yes (B) ✳   No (A)   **score** ☐ 2

10. Have you ever been to a place and felt that you have been there before?
Yes (B) ✳   No (A)   **score** ☐ 2

11. Do you believe that dreams have meaning?
Yes (B) ✳   No (A)   **score** ☐ 2

12. Do you read between the lines when you talk to people?
Yes (B) ✳   No (A)   **score** ☐ 2

54

13. Have you ever known when a telephone was about to ring?

Yes (B) ✳   No (A)   **score** 2

14. Have you ever guessed in advance what someone was about to tell you?

Yes (B) ✳   No (A)   **score** 2

15. Do you believe that you can influence the roll of a die?

Yes (B) ✳   No (A)   **score** 0

16. Do you sometimes say something at the exact moment someone else says it?

Yes (B) ✳   No (A)   **score** 2

17. Do you believe that animals have greater intuition than humans?

Yes (B) ✳   No (A)   **score** 2

18. Can you sense forthcoming danger?

Yes (B) ✳   No (A)   **score** 2

19. Do you believe in love at first sight?

Yes (B) ✳   No (A)   **score** 0

20. Do you ever sense hostility from people who appear to be friendly?

Yes (B) ✳   No (A)   **score** 2

21. Do you believe in mind over matter?

Yes (B) ✳   No (A)   **score** 2

22. Can you sometimes feel the emotions of someone who is not physically present?

Yes (B) ✳   No (A)   **score** 0

23. Do you feel drawn to certain people even though you don't know them well?

Yes (B) ✳   No (A)   **score** 2

24. Do you believe that twins have a special affinity?

Yes (B) ✳   No (A)   **score** 2

25. Do you have a special affinity with animals?

Yes (B) ✳   No (A)   **score** 2

26. Do you believe in the laws of probability?

Yes (A) ✳   No (B)   **score** 0

27. Can you sometimes foretell the future?

Yes (B) ✳   No (A)   **score** 0

28. Would you go to a fortune-teller?

Yes (B) ✳   No (A)   **score** 2

29. Are you sometimes aware of unspoken undercurrents in social situations?

Yes (B) ✳   No (A)   **score** 2

30. Do you often guess the end of a story before you have reached it?

Yes (B) ✳   No (A)   **score** 2

31. Do you believe in reincarnation?

Yes (B) ✳   No (A)   **score** 1

32. Do you believe that cats are more sensitive than human beings?

Yes (B) ✳   No (A)   **score** 2

33. Do you believe that dogs can recognize their masters by their footsteps?

Yes (B) ✳   No (A)   **score** 2

34. Can you sense when someone is behind you even though you cannot see or hear them?

Yes (B) ✳   No (A)   **score** 2

35. Do your dreams ever come true?

Yes (B) ✳   No (A)   **score** 0

36. Can you sometimes guess a person's occupation without any real clues?

Yes (B) ✳   No (A)   **score** 0

37. Do odd coincidences regularly happen in your life?

Yes (B) ✳   No (A)   **score** 0

38. Do you ever wish for something to happen?

Yes (B) ✳   No (A)   **score** 2

39. Would you enjoy the work of a psychotherapist?

Yes (B) ✳   No (A)   **score** 0

40. Do you sometimes feel that facts merely cloud an issue?

Yes (B) ✳   No (A)   **score** 0

41. Would you trust your intuition even in a very important matter where a mistake would be serious?

Yes (B) ✳   No (A)   **score** 2

42. Do you know when it is going to rain?

Yes (B) ✳   No (A)   **score** 0

43. Do you sometimes think of friends at the same moment they think of you?

Yes (B) ✳   No (A)   **score** 0

44. Do you believe in natural medicines?

Yes (B) ✳   No (A)   **score** 2

45. Do you believe in divination by Tarot cards, I Ching, etc?

Yes (B) ✳   No (A)   **score** 2

46. Do you sometimes know the sender of a letter without looking?

Yes (B) ✳   No (A)   **score** 2

47. Do you believe in the supernatural?

Yes (B) ✳   No (A)   **score** [2]

48. Can you sense when people disagree with you even if they may be trying to hide it?

Yes (B) ✳   No (A)   **score** [2]

49. Do you rely on your intuition in many different circumstances?

Yes (B) ✳   No (A)   **score** [2]

50. Do you believe that animals can sense forthcoming earthquakes?

Yes (B) ✳   No (A)   **score** [0]

SCORING KEY

A = 0 points

✳ = 1 points

B = 2 points

81 – 100
Extremely powerful intuition.
61 – 80
Strong intuitive feeling.
41 – 60
Average intuitive ability.
21 – 40
Very down to earth.
0 – 20
No intuition apparent.

How did you do? If you scored very highly on the intuition scale, then you are the sort of person for whom the 'feel' of an individual or situation is of paramount importance. You pay great attention to the non-verbal signals that everyone gives out, even when these are received only at a subliminal level. Most intuitive people talk about this faculty rather as though they possessed sensitive feelers, like those of certain insects, that can detect very slight changes in their environment. The down side of being highly intuitive is that you may be less observant of facts than other people. You may also find it hard to convince people of the validity of your feelings when forced to concede that they are 'only' based on intuition. If you are a low scorer then all this talk of intuition will just make you annoyed. You will feel that you are a practical person with no time for flights of fancy. Although you will be far more likely to give due regard to the facts of a situation, you may well miss out on subtleties and nuances that more intuitive people would easily notice.

ARE YOU DRIVEN?

Some psychologists are fond of referring to something called 'Type A behavior'. What they mean is the sort of hard-driving, impatient, irascible behaviour often displayed by people in positions of authority. Although it is not inevitable that a Type A person should be the boss, it is quite likely because such people push themselves, and are thus often highly successful. However, there is a penalty to be paid for this Type A behavior: it goes hand in hand with high levels of stress. This particular trait has been labeled 'the heart attack profile' because it was thought that those who exhibited such behavior were at increased risk of coronary illness (more recently, it has been suggested that heart disease is a risk only if the subject also exhibits high levels of animosity). Try the following questions to discover just how you rate on the Type A scale.

1. Do you tend to drive too fast?
a. Often.　**b.** Never.　**c.** Sometimes.
score ☐

2. Do you get impatient with other drivers?
a. Occasionally.　**b.** Regularly.　**c.** Never.
score 2

3. Would you try to push ahead of others?
a. No.　**b.** Yes.　**c.** Unsure.　**score** ☐

4. Are you willing to wait patiently for what you want?
a. Yes.　**b.** Unsure.　**c.** No.　**score** ☐

5. Do you set high standards of achievement for yourself?
a. Sometimes.　**b.** Always.　**c.** Never.
score 2

6. Do you suffer fools gladly?
a. Never.　**b.** Sometimes.　**c.** Usually.
score 2

7. Do you lose your temper when frustrated?
a. Not really.　**b.** Yes.　**c.** Sometimes.
score 2

8. Do you bang doors shut?
a. Often.　**b.** Sometimes.　**c.** Never.
score 1

9. Can you relax easily after a day's work?
a. Yes.　**b.** No.　**c.** Sometimes. **score** 1

10. Do you take your work troubles home with you?
a. Often.　**b.** Occasionally.　**c.** Seldom.
score 1

58

11. Are you quite happy to let others go in front of you?

a. No. **b.** Yes. **c.** Maybe. **score** `2`

12. Do you yell at other drivers because you get impatient?

a. Occasionally. **b.** Never. **c.** Often.

score `1`

13. Do you get to work early and leave late?

a. No. **b.** Yes. **c.** Occasionally. **score** `1`

14. Do you feel there are not enough hours in the day to get everything done?

a. Occasionally. **b.** Often. **c.** Seldom.

score `1`

15. Do you take all your annual holiday?

a. Always. **b.** Sometimes. **c.** Never.

score `2`

16. Do you aspire to a senior management job?

a. Yes. **b.** No. **c.** Unsure. **score** `3`

17. Are you impatient to succeed?

a. Sometimes. **b.** Yes. **c.** No. **score** `1`

18. Do you enjoy spending time with your friends and family?

a. Usually. **b.** Always. **c.** Seldom.

score `1`

19. Do you have lots of hobbies?

a. Yes. **b.** No. **c.** A few. **score** `3`

20. Do you (or did you) play sports that require aggression?

a. Often. **b.** Sometimes. **c.** Never.

score `1`

21. Would you spend Sunday morning just reading the newspapers?

a. No. **b.** Yes. **c.** Maybe. **score** `1`

22. Do you suffer from high blood pressure?

a. Don't know. **b.** Yes. **c.** No. **score** `1`

23. Do you get impatient at other people's mistakes?

a. Frequently. **b.** Never. **c.** Sometimes.

score `1`

24. Are you glad when it's time to go home after a day's work?

a. Yes. **b.** No. **c.** Not especially. **score** `2`

25. Has your doctor ever told you to take it easy?

a. Often. **b.** Sometimes. **c.** Never.

score `1`

SCORING KEY

For each answer score the number of points indicated.

1. a:3, b:1, c:2	8. a:3, b:2, c:1	15. a:1, b:2, c:3	22. a:2, b:3, c:1
2. a:2, b:3, c:1	9. a:1, b:3, c:2	16. a:3, b:1, c:2	23. a:3, b:1, c:2
3. a:1, b:3, c:2	10. a:3, b:2, c:1	17. a:2, b:3, c:1	24. a:1, b:3, c:2
4. a:1, b:2, c:3	11. a:3, b:1, c:2	18. a:2, b:1, c:3	25. a:3, b:2, c:1
5. a:2, b:3, c:1	12. a:2, b:1, c:3	19. a:1, b:3, c:2	
6. a:3, b:2, c:1	13. a:1, b:3, c:2	20. a:3, b:2, c:1	
7. a:1, b:3, c:2	14. a:2, b:3, c:1	21. a:3, b:1, c:2	

Over 65

Maximum score is 75. If you scored 65 or above, you are a typical Type A: impatient and rather aggressive. You probably have a successful career, but your home life may well suffer as a result. Your impatience may put you at some risk from car accidents, and your tendency to be aggressive might provoke a similar response from others.

55–64

If you scored 55 to 64, you are almost a Type A personality and probably find relaxation the hardest thing to do. You tend to overwork and find it difficult to unwind at the end of the day. Your health could suffer because of the constant stress you live with. You would be well advised to learn how to take things a bit easier.

45–54

If you scored from 45 to 54, you are quite balanced. You have enough get up and go to get things done, but you are not so over-stressed that it is likely to affect your health. You know how to push for what you want but can back off when it is advisable to do so.

30–44

If you scored from 30 to 44, you are really quite relaxed and find all this Type A stuff a little perplexing. After all, what's the hurry?

Below 30

If you scored below 30, you are a very relaxed type who is quite happy to let others do the rushing. Ambition does not bother you much; you take time to enjoy life.

n iccolò Machiavelli was an Italian political writer at the time of the Renaissance. His book *The Prince* became notorious for its rather amoral outlook, and his name has therefore entered the language to describe people who plot, plan, calculate, pull tricky manoeuvres and trust no one but themselves. People who score highly on such a scale usually think of themselves as hard-boiled and realistic. They feel that most other people are just too naive to live. Machiavellianism may not be the most attractive personality trait, but it is widely found among people who wheel and deal for a living. A naive and trusting politician, for example, would not last long. A Machiavellian one might end up as head honcho. See how you measure up on this scale.

1. Do you assume that people have ulterior motives even if you do not know what they are?
a. Yes. **b.** No. **c.** Unsure. **score**

2. Do you check up on people to find out whether they've told you the truth?
a. Never. **b.** Sometimes. **c.** Always. **score**

3. Would you agree that virtue is really just insufficient temptation?
a. Unsure. **b.** Yes. **c.** No. **score**

4. Do you think that most people have their price?
a. No. **b.** Unsure. **c.** Yes. **score**

5. Would you make a good politician?
a. Unsure. **b.** Yes. **c.** No. **score**

6. Do you believe what you see in advertisements?
a. Never. **b.** Sometimes. **c.** Often. **score**

7. Do you regard statistics as a way of covering up lies?
a. Occasionally. **b.** Often. **c.** Seldom. **score**

8. Are there many people you would trust completely?
a. Plenty. **b.** Almost none. **c.** Quite few. **score**

9. If someone was collecting for charity, would you trust them to use the money properly?
a. Maybe. **b.** No. **c.** Yes. **score**

10. If someone is accused of a criminal offence are you inclined to believe them guilty? **a.** No. **b.** Yes. **c.** Sometimes. **score** ☐

11. Do you regard your work colleagues as friends or competitors? **a.** Competitors. **b.** Friends. **c.** In between. **score** ☐

12. Would you trust the word of a priest? **a.** Possibly. **b.** Probably. **c.** No. **score** ☐

13. Would you lie to get what you want? **a.** Yes. **b.** Unsure. **c.** No. **score** ☐

14. Do you believe that the end justifies the means? **a.** Unsure. **b.** Yes. **c.** No. **score** ☐

15. Would you trust the word of a politician? **a.** Never. **b.** Seldom. **c.** Frequently. **score** ☐

16. Do you see relations between the sexes as a battlefield? **a.** Sometimes. **b.** Always. **c.** Never. **score** ☐

17. If you read a newspaper article do you look for flaws and inaccuracies? **a.** Always. **b.** Never. **c.** Sometimes. **score** ☐

18. Will people take advantage of you if you let them? **a.** Never. **b.** Seldom. **c.** Often. **score** ☐

19. Is it better to trick someone before they do it to you? **a.** Yes. **b.** No. **c.** Unsure. **score** ☐

20. Would you pull off a smart business deal even though it was not quite honest? **a.** No. **b.** Yes. **c.** Maybe. **score** ☐

21. Do you believe that most people would help you if you were in trouble? **a.** No. **b.** Maybe. **c.** Yes. **score** ☐

22. Could you sell second-hand cars? **a.** Maybe. **b.** Yes. **c.** No. **score** ☐

23. Do you sometimes give people information calculated to mislead them? **a.** Yes. **b.** No. **c.** Maybe. **score** ☐

24. Do you pride yourself on your ability to outwit others? **a.** Sometimes. **b.** Never. **c.** Frequently. **score** ☐

25. Would you rather be thought of as smart or honest? **a.** Smart. **b.** Unsure. **c.** Honest. **score** ☐

SCORING KEY

For each answer score the number of points indicated.

1. a:3, b:1, c:2	**8.** a:1, b:3, c:2	**15.** a:3, b:2, c:1	**22.** a:2, b:3, c:1
2. a:1, b:2, c:3	**9.** a:2, b:3, c:1	**16.** a:2, b:3, c:1	**23.** a:3, b:1, c:2
3. a:2, b:3, c:1	**10.** a:1, b:3, c:2	**17.** a:3, b:1, c:2	**24.** a:2, b:1, c:3
4. a:1, b:2, c:3	**11.** a:3, b:1, c:2	**18.** a:1, b:2, c:3	**25.** a:3, b:2, c:1
5. a:2, b:3, c:1	**12.** a:2, b:1, c:3	**19.** a:3, b:1, c:2	
6. a:3, b:2, c:1	**13.** a:3, b:2, c:1	**20.** a:1, b:3, c:2	
7. a:2, b:3, c:1	**14.** a:2, b:3, c:1	**21.** a:3, b:2, c:1	

Over 65

Maximum score is 75. If you scored 65 or above you are a pretty tough nut. You don't trust other people, are prepared to lie and trick your way to what you want, and have few scruples about the methods you employ. You will either be very successful or serve time. Possibly both.

50–64

If you scored 50 to 64 Niccolò would still have cause to be proud of you. He would admire your capacity for assessing others shrewdly and not being swayed by any silly sentimentality about people's motives.

40–49

If you scored 40 to 49 you are quite tricky enough to survive in a hard world, but you do have some scruples and are not really as unscrupulous as you might think.

30–39

A score of 30 to 39 indicates that you're really something of a softie. You actually believe that others can have good motives and you are unwilling to use any means to get what you want.

20–29

A score of 20 to 29 suggests that you are a really nice person but will regularly get taken advantage of by people who do not share your sunny view of human nature.

Below 20

If you scored below 20, you are probably not safe to go out alone.

f or some people material success is the motivating force of their entire lives. They are engaged in a constant struggle to get to the top, and find this mission more important than other considerations, such as home, family and leisure pursuits. Others are quite unconcerned with climbing the greasy pole and are happy to live a more modest life in less stressful circumstances. Which are you? The following test should help you decide.

1. Did you know what career you wanted even when you were still at school?
a. Yes. **b.** No. **c.** Not sure. **score** ☐

2. Do you agree that 'the best things in life are free'?
a. Yes. **b.** Unsure. **c.** No. **score** ☐

3. Is winning important to you?
a. Unsure. **b.** Yes. **c.** No. **score** ☐

4. Do you work more than you have to?
a. No. **b.** Unsure. **c.** Yes. **score** ☐

5. Do you feel you need a high salary?
a. Yes. **b.** Perhaps. **c.** No. **score** ☐

6. Have you got your next promotion planned?
a. No. **b.** Yes. **c.** Unsure. **score** ☐

7. Would you make a good ship's captain?
a. Unsure. **b.** No. **c.** Yes. **score** ☐

8. Would you accept a lower salary if you could spend more time with your family?
a. Yes. **b.** No. **c.** Unsure. **score** ☐

9. Would you compete with a friend for promotion even though it might endanger your relationship?
a. Yes. **b.** Unsure. **c.** No. **score** ☐

10. Do you long to emulate successful people?
a. No. **b.** Unsure. **c.** Yes. **score** ☐

11. Do you feel discontented with your current level of prosperity?
a. Unsure. **b.** No. **c.** Yes. **score** ☐

12. Do you have a game plan for the development of your career?
a. Yes. **b.** Unsure. **c.** No. **score** ☐

13. Would you take a day off on the spur of the moment?
a. Yes. **b.** Unsure. **c.** No. **score** ☐

14. Do you admire people who are ruthless in pursuit of success?
a. Yes. **b.** No. **c.** Unsure. **score** ☐

15. Would you agree that 'the love of money is the root of all evil'?
a. Unsure. **b.** Yes. **c.** No. **score** ☐

16. Do you enjoy the luxuries that money can buy?
a. No. **b.** Yes. **c.** Unsure. **score** ☐

17. Who do you admire more, Madonna or Mahatma Gandhi?
a. Madonna. **b.** Gandhi. **c.** Unsure. **score** ☐

18. Do you like to spend time messing about in the garden?
a. Yes. **b.** No. **c.** Unsure. **score** ☐

19. Do you think about your work much during your free time?
a. Sometimes. **b.** Often. **c.** Seldom. **score** ☐

20. Is status of much concern to you?
a. No. **b.** Yes. **c.** Unsure. **score** ☐

21. Is it important to you to drive a new, powerful car?
a. Unsure. **b.** No. **c.** Yes. **score** ☐

22. Would you expect to succeed in politics?
a. Yes. **b.** Unsure. **c.** No. **score** ☐

23. Do you dream of giving up the rat race and doing something less stressful?
a. Yes. **b.** Unsure. **c.** No. **score** ☐

24. Do people regard you mainly with affection or mainly with respect?
a. Respect. **b.** Affection. **c.** Unsure. **score** ☐

25. Do you ever socialize with people just because they are useful to you?
a. No. **b.** Unsure. **c.** Yes. **score** ☐

SCORING KEY

For each answer score the number of points indicated.

1. a:3, b:1, c:2	8. a:1, b:3, c:2	15. a:2, b:1, c:3	22. a:3, b:2, c:1
2. a:1, b:2, c:3	9. a:3, b:2, c:1	16. a:1, b:3, c:2	23. a:1, c:2, b:3
3. a:2, b:3, c:1	10. a:1, b:2, c:3	17. a:3, b:1, c:2	24. a:3, b:1, c:2
4. a:1, b:2, c:3	11. a:2, b:1, c:3	18. a:1, b:3, c:2	25. a:1, b:2, c:3
5. a:3, b:2, c:1	12. a:3, b:2, c:1	19. a:2, b:3, c:1	
6. a:1, b:3, c:2	13. a:1, b:2, c:3	20. a:1, b:3, c:2	
7. a:2, b:1, c:3	14. a:3, b:1, c:2	21. a:2, b:1, c:3	

Over 65

Maximum score is 75. If you scored 65 or above, ambition is clearly of the greatest importance to you. You are the sort of person who will succeed or die!. You may find that other areas of your life are fairly empty, but though you may have cause for some regret, you will always feel that you have carried out your mission to succeed.

50–64

In this range, you are still quite ambitious and will spend most of your time trying to make your career a success. In spite of your success, you might have regrets about things you have left undone.

40–49

In this range, you are quite keen on your career but by no means obsessed with it.

You want to do well, but think that there is more to life than getting ahead.

30–44

In this range, ambition does not mean that much to you. You enjoy other aspects of your life just as much, and are willing to accept a lower standard of living if you can be happy.

20–29

In this range, you are really not ambitious at all. You value your free time and have many things you would rather do than struggle for material gain. You are not very status-conscious and cannot understand what makes people struggle so hard succeed.

Below 30

If you scored below 20 you probably have no idea what ambition means.

the ability to concentrate is vital in all areas of life. Whether you are working, studying, playing sport or driving your car you need to be able to keep your mind on the job in hand. Many people find this difficult. They have a tendency to daydream even in circumstances where this could be dangerous. Test your own powers of concentration.

1. When ploughing through a difficult read, do you:

		score
a.	Often find that you have to re-read a page because you didn't take any of it in.	✓
b.	Take it slowly, stopping every few pages to ensure you know what's going on.	
c.	Generally read a generous chunk before feeling your attention is lapsing.	

2. You're gazing out of the window during a long train journey. When considering what scenery you've just pass by, do you:

		score
a.	Feel able to describe much of the landscape you've just passed through.	
b.	Discover you drifted off and have no idea where you are.	✓
c.	Have vague notions of the sights you've just witnessed, but in no particular order.	

3. During a heated discussion, you find yourself embroiled in a complicated argument. Are you most likely to:

		score
a.	Lose your train of thought and stop to ask, 'Where was I?'	✓
b.	Follow the argument closely, and stick to the subject matter rigidly.	
c.	Lose interest after the first few exchanges of ideas.	

4. You're confronted with a lengthy logic puzzle. Do you:

		score
a.	Attempt to solve it but put it aside when your brain refuses to function after the first ten minutes of intense thought.	✓
b.	Persevere purposefully until it's fully solved.	
c.	Have to refocus your thoughts on the problem in hand when you find your mind is wandering.	

5. After sitting through a rather tedious documentary, do you usually find:

		score
a.	You've forgotten most of what you've just witnessed.	✓
b.	You can quote a detailed synopsis of the contents to interested friends later.	

6. You stop to ask a passer-by directions to the street you're searching for. After a rather lengthy explanation of the route, are you most likely to:

		score
a.	Set off in eager anticipation, and find the required street without further ado.	
b.	Manage to follow the correct route for a short while before forgetting the next stage and having to ask someone else for directions.	
c.	Admit you didn't quite get all that, and request the passer-by to kindly repeat it all.	✓

7. Half an hour through a rather banal meeting with colleagues, you realize you're being asked a question. Would you generally:

		score
a.	Have to ask them to repeat the question.	
b.	Throw together an answer which you hope fully answers the question you only half heard.	✓
c.	Launch into an answer that directly relates to the topic of concern.	

8. You're given a somewhat daunting project to conduct. Are you most likely to complete it:

		score
a.	In dribs and drabs, picking it up every now and again, and pushing it aside when you get bored.	
b.	Efficiently by structuring your work carefully, and sticking to your schedule without further procrastination.	
c.	Just on time, having found it easier to sit down and focus as the deadline approaches.	

9. During a casual stroll to the local shop, a neighbor approaches and you stop for a chat. Are you most likely to:

		score
a.	Literally bump into your neighbor before you realize it's her.	
b.	Spot her before she spots you.	
c.	Greet each other simultaneously.	

10. Background music is filtering into your work area, where you're trying to solve a complex problem. Are you most likely to find yourself:

		score
a.	So focused you're not even aware of the music.	
b.	Distracted totally and in need of a break.	
c.	Conscious of the interference but able to focus on your work.	

11. Halfway through reading a rather convoluted legal document, you're interrupted by a friend who asks if you fancy a break. Would you:

		score
a.	Stop willingly as your attention was drifting anyway.	
b.	Prefer to plough on as you'd like to get through it without being distracted.	
c.	Be in need of another break despite your previous two.	

12. When browsing through newspapers, do you find yourself:

		score
a.	Not really absorbing much of what you've read.	
b.	Wincing at all the grammatical errors you spot during your perusals.	
c.	Able to quote the major news of the day back to others afterwards.	

13. A relative is chatting amicably to you as you prepare some supper. Would you:

		score
a.	Be able to conduct a coherent conversation while cooking up a tasty meal.	
b.	Find yourself unable to do both at once, taking twice as long to prepare the food.	
c.	Mutter a few token acknowledgements to your relative while re-reading the recipe you've been distracted from.	

14. Do you find deadlines:

score

a.	Difficult to meet, as you find it hard to consistently focus on the task.	
b.	A useful incentive – when you know when you've got to have something finished by a certain date, you find it relatively easy to get it done.	
c.	Normally unnecessary as you find yourself suitably motivated to settle down on a task and get it finished promptly without them.	

15. During an energetic bicycle ride, a pedestrian suddenly blocks your path. Are you most likely to have:

score

a.	Seen the pedestrian from some distance and slowed down accordingly.	
b.	Been rather rudely awoken from your da-dream and had to swerve to avoid calamity.	
c.	Slammed on your brakes just in time as you realized what was about to happen.	

16. Your mind wanders during a dreary talk you're attending. Do you find yourself:

score

a.	Unaware of your daydreaming until a sharp prod from your neighbor jolts you back to reality.	
b.	Able to refocus your attention quickly on the talk in progress.	
c.	Attempting in vain to focus, but quickly drifting off into your daydream again.	

17. Two chums sit down behind you on the bus and engage in an animated chat. Is your attempt to read the latest blockbuster likely to be:

score

a.	A dismal failure as you tune in to the juicy gossip being regaled behind you.	
b.	A success: you remain totally engrossed in your novel.	
c.	A challenge – you find yourself having to re-read a paragraph every now and again.	

18. Do you find simple sums:

		score
a.	Calculable mentally if no noisy distractions abound.	
b.	Impossible to do in your head as you always get distracted by something else.	
c.	Easy enough to calculate mentally – you can block distractions out.	

19. A hectic morning presents you with a multitude of urgent tasks. Do you:

		score
a.	Prioritize, concentrating entirely on one task at a time, working through the list methodically.	
b.	Switch constantly between tasks, unable to focus entirely on any particular thing.	
c.	Attempt to address the different problems in turn, but remaining somewhat distracted by unresolved tasks during the course of your work.	

20. Do long lists of instructions generally leave you:

		score
a.	Informed and capable – you find yourself able to assimilate large chunks of information in a short time.	
b.	Rather muddled – you tend to get distracted during attempts to absorb instructions of a complex nature.	
c.	As uninformed as before – you're unlikely to even attempt to digest such wads of information in one sitting.	

21. At the end of a lengthy film boasting an intricate plot, are you likely to be the one:

		score
a.	Others ask what happens as they've drifted off while you've remained alert.	
b.	Who has 'switched off' frequently throughout, annoying the others with constant pleas for explanations.	
c.	Who can generally establish the basic plot, though exact details often fall by the wayside.	

22. Would you tend to ascribe any failure to remember news someone has told you to:

score

a.	The fact that you weren't concentrating on what was said at the time.	
b.	Your poor memory – you were paying attention, but time eroded the memory and replaced it with something else.	
c.	A freak occurrence – you generally possess a competent degree of focus and retention.	

23. An unwelcome telephone call brings you the bad personal news you've been dreading. Next day do you find yourself:

score

a.	Wandering around in a daze unable to concentrate on anything.	
b.	Eager to find things demanding of your attention to take your mind off it.	
c.	Attempting to be distracted by jobs that need doing, but failing to focus wholeheartedly on the job in hand.	

24. A mild cold leaves you blocked up and miserable. Do you find your favorite magazine to be:

score

a.	A welcome distraction – you try and succeed in refocusing your concentration positively.	
b.	No help – you're determined to dwell on your discomfort and refuse to concentrate on anything.	
c.	A comfort, but your usual listlessness is exacerbated and you find it tough concentrating on anything for long.	

25. After a particularly gruelling day in the office, you attempt to hail a taxi in rush hour. Are your efforts:

score

a.	Futile – you're hindered by thoughts of the day, which distract your search for a cab.	
b.	Successful – you're focused on your search for a taxi, and will conduct a post mortem on your day later.	
c.	Promising until a scuffle breaks out across the road and your attention lapses momentarily, losing you that elusive taxi.	

SCORING KEY

For each answer score the number of points indicated.

1. a:3, b:1, c:2	**8.** a:1, b:2, c:3	**15.** a:1, b:2, c:3	**22.** a:1, b:3, c:2
2. a:3, b:2, c:1	**9.** a:2, b:3:c:1	**16.** a:1, b:2, c:3	**23.** a:1, b:2, c:3
3. a:3, b:2, c:1	**10.** a:3, b:2, c:1	**17.** a:1, b:3, c:2	**24.** a:1, b:3, c:2
4. a:2, b:3, c:1	**11.** a:3, b:1, c:2	**18.** a:1, b:2, c:3	**25:** a:2, b:1, c:3.
5. a:2, b:3, c:1	**12.** a:2, b:3, c:1	**19.** a:3, b:1, c:2	
6. a:2, b:3, c:1	**13.** a:3, b:1, c:2	**20.** a:1, b:3, c:2	
7. a:2, b:3, c:1	**14.** a:3, b:1, c:2	**21.** a:1, b:3, c:2	

A score in the high 40s suggests you are someone capable of focusing on the engrossing task at hand even if a frenzy of clucking chickens flutters past your desk. 35 and above is fairly average, with gripping activities claiming your attention until something more interesting or newer comes along. Easing down into the 20s suggests a concentration level more akin to a toddler's. You're in need of constant flashing lights, excitement and change, as your attention span is largely momentary. Below that and you stand little chance of ever achieving very much without a great deal of re-reading and huffing and puffing. You're more an expert in breaks than the art of study.

this is a test of both physical and moral courage. In each situation you are given three choices of action and you must choose only one. Keep a note of your choices and compare them with the scoring key at the end of the test.

1. You see a child in difficulty at the swimming pool. You are not that good a swimmer yourself, but the situation seems desperate. Do you:

		score
a.	Jump in any way and hope that you will be able to cope.	
b.	Run for the lifeguard even though it might be too late when you get back.	
c.	Try to throw the child a rope.	

2. You're taking a walk in the country when you pass a farmyard guarded by fierce dogs. To your horror they are able to get out of the yard, and run towards you growling and barking. Do you:

		score
a.	Shout at them to sit down.	
b.	Freeze.	
c.	Run.	

3. You have taken important exams but do not feel confident about the results. When the dreaded letter comes do you:

		score
a.	Open it immediately to see the worst.	
b.	Get someone else to open it and read it to you.	
c.	Put off opening it until later.	

4. You witness an armed robbery in progress. Do you:

		score
a.	Run to call the police.	
b.	Try to apprehend the criminals yourself.	
c.	Hide in a nearby shop until the danger is past.	

5. You are driving and you see a truck weaving dangerously along the road ahead. The driver is either ill or drunk. Do you:

		score
a.	Pull in and call the police.	
b.	Flash your lights and try to get the driver to stop.	
c.	Keep well back out of danger.	

6. Your mother-in-law keeps interfering in your marriage until the point where you have finally had as much as you can take. However, she is known for her fearsome temper. Do you:

		score
a.	Try to explain tactfully that her attitude is causing problems.	
b.	Let her have it. Pour out in one torrent all the anger and frustration of the last 10 years.	
c.	Think better of it and go outside to chop some wood while you calm down.	

7. You take your kids swimming. The other parents are all diving and your kids want you to join in, but you've never done it before. Do you:

		score
a.	Explain that you don't feel confident enough to dive.	
b.	Shut your eyes and chuck yourself off the diving board	
c.	Make an excuse that you aren't feeling well.	

8. You go with your partner to a congress in Tokyo. You don't speak a word of Japanese and you have never visited the city before. While your partner is involved in business, do you:

		score
a.	Stay in the hotel and amuse yourself as best you can.	
b.	Take a guided tour.	
c.	Set out to explore the city on your own.	

9. You are taking part in an amateur dramatic production when the star is suddenly taken ill. Horror of horrors, the understudy has failed to turn up as well! You know the part backwards though you have never performed it, being new to the company and having only a small role. Do you:

		score
a.	Keep quiet and let them find someone who can muddle through.	
b.	Announce confidently that you will save the day.	
c.	Mention casually that you have read the part and hope that they will beg you to give it a try.	

10. You suffer from arachnophobia. You are alone in the house when you come across a huge spider. Do you:

		score
a.	Beat it to death with something heavy.	
b.	Master your fear and, having trapped it in a glass, throw it out of the window.	
c.	Rush out of the house and refuse to return until someone comes home who can catch the spider.	

11. At a meeting of your school's PTA you are appalled to hear a friend of yours accused behind her back of being a bad parent. Do you:

		score
a.	Loudly stand up for your friend in front of the other parents.	
b.	Say nothing.	
c.	Keep quiet at the meeting but tell your friend privately what you heard.	

12. Your child is terrified of dental treatment, a fear that you share. However, she needs an appointment with the dentist. Do you:

		score
a.	Sit with her and try to comfort her while the dentist is at work.	
b.	Let her watch you having your treatment first to give her encouragement.	
c.	Push her into the surgery and retire to the waiting room hoping for the best.	

13. On an office outing everyone decides to have a go on a white-knuckle ride. Do you:

a.	Jump at the idea enthusiastically and encourage others to join in the fun.	
b.	Remember something you have left behind and rush off to look for it.	
c.	Grit your teeth and have a go even though you're terrified.	

14. You and your family are flying home from holiday when the plane runs into bad weather. The turbulence is the worst you have ever experienced and everyone is terrified the plane will crash. Do you:

score

a.	Remain calm and try to encourage your family to do the same.	
b.	Clutch your loved ones to you and wait helplessly for the end.	
c.	Find a stewardess and ask her for reassurance that everything will be all right.	

15. You are ill and suspect that your condition may be serious despite what the doctors tell you. Do you:

score

a.	Make yourself believe your doctors.	
b.	Ask a close relative for 'the truth' even though you are aware they are unlikely to give it.	
c.	Demand that the doctors tell you the worst.	

16. You awake in the night to hear a noise downstairs. You think you may have burglars. Do you:

score

a.	Barricade the bedroom door and stay quiet until they have gone.	
b.	Tiptoe downstairs and attempt to phone the police without being overheard.	
c.	Take a heavy stick and charge downstairs to sort them out.	

17. You run into serious debt and the bank manager summons you to explain. Do you:

score

a.	Keep making excuses to avoid a meeting.	
b.	Meet him, explain the situation fully and ask what he will do to help.	
c.	Meet him and grovel.	

18. You see a crowd of white youths surrounding some black kids and shouting threats and racist taunts. Do you:

		score
a.	Cross the road and walk away.	
b.	Go to find a police officer.	
c.	Shout at the crowd to stop what they are doing.	

19. You go deep-sea fishing. To your amazement you find you've hooked a large shark. Do you:

		score
a.	Fight it to your very last breath.	
b.	Cut it loose as quickly as possible.	
c.	Make a token effort to land it but feel secretly relieved when it gets away.	

20. While trying to get on a bus you are pushed out of the way by a man who's much bigger than you. Do you:

		score
a.	Take a step back to avoid a confrontation.	
b.	Push your way in front of him and risk a fight.	
c.	Point out to him politely that you were ahead of him.	

21. New neighbors move in next door, and you soon discover just how much they enjoy loud music. Do you:

		score
a.	Ignore it and hope that they will improve with time.	
b.	Walk right round to their front door and complain.	
c.	Take an opportunity to bump into them as though by accident and point out tactfully that the music is too loud.	

22. You work as a research scientist and have been pursuing your pet project for 20 years. To your dismay a piece of evidence turns up that completely undermines all your work. Do you:

score

a.	Pretend that the evidence does not exist and carry on as though nothing had happened.	
b.	Write to a leading scientific journal and announce the failure of your project quoting the evidence in full.	
c.	Keep working and try to uncover other evidence that would be more acceptable.	

23. Driving on a lonely road at night you accidentally run over and kill a tramp. Do you:

score

a.	Drive on. Nobody is going to make a big fuss about a dead tramp anyway.	
b.	Drive to the nearest town and call the police anonymously.	
c.	Find a phone, summon the police and take responsibility for the accident.	

24. Looking through old papers, you discover your birth certificate which reveals that you were adopted. Your adoptive parents are now elderly and clearly intended that you should never know the facts of your birth. Do you:

score

a.	Put the paper back and pretend you never found it.	
b.	Go straight to your adoptive parents and demand the facts.	
c.	Hint gently that you have some misgivings about your origins and hope that they decide to explain.	

25. Your son asks you about your involvement in a long-distant war. The truth is that you dodged the draft because you were scared. Do you:

score

a.	Say you refused to go as a matter of principle.	
b.	Lie about your military career.	
c.	Tell the truth and explain that war is something people should be scared of.	

SCORING KEY

For each answer score the number of points indicated.

1. a:3, b:1, c:2	**8.** a:1, b:2, c:3	**15.** a:1, b:2, c:3	**22.** a:1, b:3, c:2
2. a:3, b:2, c:1	**9.** a:2, b:3:c:1	**16.** a:1, b:2, c:3	**23.** a:1, b:2, c:3
3. a:3, b:2, c:1	**10.** a:3, b:2, c:1	**17.** a:1, b:3, c:2	**24.** a:1, b:3, c:2
4. a:2, b:3, c:1	**11.** a:3, b:1, c:2	**18.** a:1, b:2, c:3	**25:** a:2, b:1, c:3.
5. a:2, b:3, c:1	**12.** a:2, b:3, c:1	**19.** a:3, b:1, c:2	
6. a:2, b:3, c:1	**13.** a:3, b:1, c:2	**20.** a:1, b:3, c:2	
7. a:2, b:3, c:1	**14.** a:3, b:1, c:2	**21.** a:1, b:3, c:2	

70s

The maximum score for this test is 75 points. The minimum is 25. If you scored in the 70s, you are exceptionally brave in almost all circumstances. Your bravery covers the entire spectrum of moral and physical courage and is truly admirable. However, with such a strong tendency to plunge head first into dangerous situations, your chances of living a long life are probably less impressive.

60s

If you scored in the 60s, you are still very brave but have also learned a certain amount of discretion. You do not just plunge in regardless but tend to think a little before you act.

50s

If you scored in the 50s, you are probably about average.

ow much do you worry about your health? Are you the sort of person who only has to hear the symptoms of a disease to believe that you suffer from it, or is your doctor a stranger to you? Try the following quick test to see how you measure up as a hypochondriac.

1. Do you sometimes suspect you may have an ulcer?

a. Yes. **b.** No. **c.** Undecided. **score**

2. You read in the newspapers that people with gum disease are more likely to have heart attacks. Do you:

		score
a.	Shrug it off as another crazy health scare.	
b.	Resolve to take more notice of dental hygiene.	
c.	Make an appointment to see your dentist straight away.	

3. Your partner notices that your hair is thinning. Do you:

		score
a.	Take no notice – these things happen as you get older.	
b.	Spend a lot of money on the latest fashionable remedy..	
c.	Take up massaging your scalp in the hope that it helps.	

4. Do you weigh yourself frequently?

a. Yes. **b.** No. **c.** Undecided. **score**

5. Do you examine your tongue often?

a. Yes. **b.** No. **c.** Undecided. **score**

6. You read that frequent teeth-cleaning is an important part of staying healthy. Do you:

		score
a.	Start to clean your teeth three times a day.	
b.	Make no change to your current regimen.	
c.	Resolve to clean your teeth better in future.	

7. You see something on television about the benefits of eating oily fish. Do you:

		score
a.	Take no notice – you don't much like fish.	
b.	Make sure you eat it regularly.	
c.	Decide you might eat it when you remember.	

8. If you were to get palpitations, would you:

		score
a.	Assume you were suffering from heart disease.	
b.	Decide you were stressed and needed a holiday.	
c.	Not worry about the cause.	

9. If a friend recommended a faith healer would you:

		score
a.	Dismiss the whole thing as nonsense.	
b.	Wonder whether there might be something in it.	
c.	Make a careful note of the details for future use.	

10. An expert suggests that you should have a first-aid box in your car. Do you:

		score
a.	Ignore the suggestion.	
b.	Think it's a good idea but never get round to buying one.	
c.	Go and buy one straightaway and make sure it is always in place.	

11. If someone says that you seem to have lost weight recently, do you:

		score
a.	Accept it as a compliment.	
b.	Wonder what could have caused the weight loss.	
c.	Assume that you must be ill.	

12. Do you get dizzy turns?

a. Never.   **b.** Sometimes.   **c.** Frequently.   **score**

13. Do you consider yourself to be a healthy person?

		score
a.	Yes, I'm never ill.	
b.	I try not to bother the doctor.	
c.	I've had health problems all my life.	

14. Do you follow a diet:

a. Always.   **b.** When I get a bit overweight.   **c.** Never.   **score**

15. Do you watch medical documentaries on television?

a. Avidly.   **b.** Occasionally.   **c.** Seldom.   **score**

16. Do you consult a 'Family Doctor' book about your symptoms?

a. Regularly.   **b.** Occasionally.   **c.** Never.   **score**

17. Do you carry painkillers on your person just in case you are ill?

a. Never.   **b.** Sometimes.   **c.** Always.   **score**

18. When you think of your old age, do you:

		score
a.	Assume that you will have a few problems but remain reasonably healthy.	
b.	Fear that you will become incapacitated and dependent upon others.	
c.	Never give the matter any thought.	

19. You notice a strange spot on your skin that you have not seen before. Do you:

		score
a.	Take no notice – after all, it's only a spot.	
b.	Keep it under observation to see if it changes.	
c.	Rush to the doctor to tell him you suspect malignant melanoma.	

20. When eating out do you:

		score
a.	Worry whether the kitchen staff have washed their hands before touching the food.	
b.	Forget about health – you're here to enjoy the meal.	
c.	Only go to a place whose reputation you are happy with.	

21. Are you afraid of coming into contact with infectious diseases?

		score
a.	Not at all.	
b.	Only in areas where disease is widespread.	
c.	Always.	

22. Do you get constipated for no apparent reason?

a. Often.   **b.** Never.   **c.** Seldom.   **score**

23. Do you check your pulse?

a. Occasionally.   **b.** Frequently.   **c.** Never.   **score**

24. Do you take vitamins?

a. Always.   **b.** Never.   **c.** Sometimes.   **score**

25. Do you worry about your health?

a. Quite frequently.   **b.** Only occasionally.   **c.** Almost never.   **score**

SCORING KEY

For each answer score the number of points indicated.

1. a:3, b:1, c:2	**8.** a:3, b:2, c:1	**15.** a:3, b:2, c:1	**22.** a:3, b:1, c:2
2. a:1, b:2, c:3	**9.** a:1, b:2, c:3	**16.** a:3, b:2, c:1	**23.** a:3, b:2, c:1
3. a:1, b:3, c:2	**10.** a:1, b:2, c:3	**17.** a:1, c:2, b:3	**24.** a:3, b:1, c:2
4. a:3, b:1, c:2	**11.** a:1, b:2, c:3	**18.** a:2, b:3, c:1	**25.** a:3, b:2, c:1
5. a:3, b:1, c:2	**12.** a:1, b:2, c:3	**19.** a:1, b:2, c:3	
6. a:3, b:1, c:2	**13.** a:1, b:2, c:3	**20.** a:3, b:1, c:2	
7. a:1, b:3, c:2	**14.** a:3, b:2, c:1	**21.** a:1, b:2, c:3	

Over 60

Most of us imagine illnesses at some time or other, but if this becomes a habit it may well point to deep anxieties that have not been recognized and dealt with. If you have a score of over 60 (the maximum is 75), you have a problem. For once the answer might really be to seek the help of your doctor.

50s

A score in the 50s would suggest that you worry about your health quite a lot. Certainly you seem preoccupied with the idea that you may become ill.

40s

A score in the 40s is rather more realistic, although you still sometimes harbor unjustified concerns over your health. to be bit more positive about your health.

30s

A score in the 30s suggests that you have no real health worries but are sensible enough to recognize when there may be a genuine problem.

Below 29

A score below 29 would suggest that you are definitely no hypochondriac; you do not take your health very seriously; if you have a problem, it may be that you ignore vital early warning signals of impending illness.

Select the (*one*) answer that most applies to you in each of the 25 questions.

1. Do you feel most relaxed when:

		score
a.	You are just in your own company.	
b.	You are with two or three family and friends.	
c.	You are at a fairly large social gathering.	

2. At a social function you are standing in a group of 4 to 5 people. Do you usually:

		score
a.	Do most of the listening to the others' conversation.	
b.	Contribute to the conversation equally with the others.	
c.	Usually make all the running in the conversation.	

3. When communicating with someone on a one-to-one basis, do you feel more comfortable communicating by:

a. Letter.   **b.** Telephone.   **c.** Face to face.   **score** [ ]

4. You are on a bus or train. Do you:

		score
a.	Never start up a conversation with a stranger sitting next to you or opposite.	
b.	Occasionally start a conversation with them.	
c.	Usually start up some sort of conversation.	

5. You are walking down the street and someone is coming towards you who you vaguely recognize. Do you:

		score
a.	Walk past and ignore them unless they speak to you.	
b.	Give them a glance and sort of half nod.	
c.	Speak to them and attempt to engage them in some sort of conversation to find out how you know them.	

6. Would you take part in a karaoke competition?

a. You must be joking.   **b.** Maybe.   **c.** Just try and stop me.   **score** ☐

7. How often do you tell jokes in the company of others?

a. Never.   **b.** Sometimes.   **c.** Often.   **score** ☐

8. How often do you speak at meetings?

a. Hardly ever.   **b.** Sometimes.   **c.** Very often.   **score** ☐

9. Do you ever chat up the opposite sex?

a. Never.   **b.** Occasionally.   **c.** Often.   **score** ☐

10. Would you ever take part in an amateur stage production?

a. No way.   **b.** I might if pressed.   **c.** Yes, I would love to.   **score** ☐

11. When meeting someone for the first time do you:

		score
a.	Feel awkward and nervous.	
b.	Feel at ease and interested in getting to know them.	
c.	Feel bursting to tell them all about yourself.	

12. At the end of a dinner party when saying goodbye to a guest of the opposite sex would you prefer to:

		score
a.	Just shake their hand.	
b.	Shake their hand and pat them on the arm.	
c.	Shake their hand and kiss them on both cheeks.	

13. When having a one-to-one conversation with someone would you prefer to:

		score
a.	Listen to them talking about what they have been doing recently.	
b.	Talk equally about what each of you have been doing.	
c.	Tell them mainly about what you have been doing.	

14. You are in a crowded lift. Do you:

		score
a.	Keep yourself to yourself and hardly notice the other people.	
b.	Don't say much but usually have a good look at the people in the lift with you.	
c.	Usually try to make some witty remark to the other people in the lift	

15. At a work-sponsored dinner you are sitting at the table with 20 other people. How much conversation do you make?

		score
a.	I speak very little but listen to other people and get on with my meal.	
b.	Usually I speak mainly just to the people on either side of me.	
c.	I do tend to make quite a bit of the general conversation round the table.	

16. You are walking along in the town centre and a television station is conducting random interviews with people on a certain topic. Do you:

		score
a.	Turn in the other direction or cross over to the other side of the street to ignore them.	
b.	Say a few words for the camera if approached.	
c.	Go out of your way to make sure that they ask you.	

17. You work in an office and the company board chairman walks through. Do you:

		score
a.	Keep you head down and hope he doesn't even notice you.	
b.	Carry on as normal and speak to him if appropriate.	
c.	Make sure that you have some sort of a conversation with him.	

18. You are attending a function at which some important and influential people will also be attending. What would you wear?

		score
a.	What I would normally wear to any other function.	
b.	I would probably buy something new for the occasion.	
c.	I would make sure I wore something to make me stand out from the crowd.	

19. How often do you push for promotion at work?

a. Never.   **b.** Sometimes.   **c.** Often.   **score** ⬚

20. How would you feel if asked to make a speech in front of a large group?

score

a.	Terrified at the prospect.	
b.	I would try to prepare and make a good job of it even though it was not something that I would choose to do.	
c.	I would be pleased and excited at the prospect.	

21. Do you sunbathe in your swimwear in the back garden in view of the neighbors?

a. Never.   **b.** Occasionally.   **c.** Often.   **score** ⬚

22. You are at a club and the singer asks for volunteers to go up on stage to help him out with a number. Would you:

a. Never ever volunteer.   **b.** Might possibly volunteer.   **c.** Be up on stage in a flash.   **score** ⬚

23. When you are worried about something do you:

score

a.	Bottle it up inside you.	
b.	Discuss it with close friends and family.	
c.	Discuss it with as many people as you can.	

24. If you are in the company of people who start telling risqué jokes how do you react?

score

a.	I feel very embarrassed and wish they would shut up.	
b.	I don't particularly approve but am not embarrassed.	
c.	I match them joke for joke.	

25. If a rather loud verbal argument breaks out between two colleagues at work, do you:

score

a.	Keep you head down and leave well alone.	
b.	Perhaps try to calm things down if you think it wise to do so in the circumstances.	
c.	Almost always get involvedh either by joining in or trying to calm things down.	

SCORING KEY

Award yourself 2 points for every (c) answer, 1 point for every (b) and 0 points for every (a) answer.

40–50 points:

You are most certainly not a shrinking violet; in fact you are brimming with self-confidence. While this is not a bad thing, you should be careful at all times not to be extrovert to the point where people find you excessively pushy, even overbearing. Just remember at all times that your bubbly personality should be tempered with some degree of modesty and sensitivity toward other people.

25–39 points:

You are no shrinking violet (even though you may sometimes think you are), but at the same time you don't push yourself beyond what to most people is an acceptable degree of behavior. If you feel you are a little shy and backward at coming forward at times, it may be because you secretly admire the way more extrovert people behave. But remember that it is these people who are in the minority and that, by showing a little reserve at the right time, you are probably regarded by other people as a much more appealing personality and someone they enjoy having in their company.

Less than 25:

You are what some people would call a shrinking violet, but that's the way many people are, and it doesn't make you any worse a person than someone who is excessively outgoing. Many people are extremely modest and shy but at the same time have the ability to be high achievers in their own field providing that they can recognize their own talents and gain that bit of extra self-confidence to harness their potential. Remember that many people who appear loud and pushy are actually inwardly shy, and lack self-confidence. Their seemingly extrovert behaviour is sometimes their way of trying to overcome their own inner doubts.

1. You are faced with a number of problems at work. Do you:

a.	Go to sleep as soon as your head hits the pillow.	
b.	Lie awake half the night worrying.	
c.	Think about work for a while before going to sleep.	

2. You are going on holiday. Do you:

score

a.	Plan well ahead so you don't have to rush around just before you set off.	
b.	Rush around the day before you go, trying to get everything done in time.	
c.	Check all the bags in a frenzy, panicking in case you have forgotten something essential.	

3. You have an important interview coming up. Do you:

score

a.	Look forward to it as you enjoy interviews.	
b.	Have a tense feeling in your stomach all day and can't think of anything else.	
c.	Get on with your work as usual but feel slightly apprehensive about the forthcoming meeting.	

4. You are holding a dinner party and your guests are late. Do you:

score

a.	Get in a panic because the dinner might be spoiled.	
b.	Put the dinner on hold and sit down and relax with a drink and a magazine.	
c.	Try to keep the dinner going but feel you cannot really relax until the guests get there.	

5. Christmas is coming up and lot of things are still left to be done. Do you:

score

a.	Take things in your stride and the holiday with enthusiasm.	
b.	Lie awake at night worrying about how you can get possibly everything done in time.	
c.	Run around like a headless chicken trying to do three things at once.	

6. You are on your way to a business meeting and get stuck in a traffic jam. Do you:

score

a.	Wait calmly until it moves – after all it's not your fault that you're late.	
b.	Get rather impatient but pass the time by reading your newspaper.	
c.	Get totally overwrought and don't know how to curb your impatience.	

7. Your next-door neighbors are playing loud music. Do you:

score

a.	Take it calmly and think if it carries on you might have a quiet word with them.	
b.	Get irritated and tell your partner you cannot possibly function with this noise going on.	
c.	Try to ignore it for an hour, then when you can't stand it any longer go nextdoor shouting, 'Turn the music down!'	

8. You are invited to a large party in the evening. Do you:

score

a.	Look forward to it, as you love meeting new people.	
b.	Rush around the day before you go, trying to get everything done in time.	
c.	Carry on as normal but think it will probably be less trouble to stick with the people you know during the evening	

9. You are flying abroad on business. Do you:

score

a.	Leave two hours early and worry constantly that you might not get there in time.	
b.	Leave in good time but feel slightly apprehensive at the prospect of the journey.	
c.	Take the journey in a relaxed mood as nothing is likely to go wrong.	

10. You come home and the living room is a total mess. Do you:

score

a.	Get irritated by it and shout at everybody to tidy it up immediately.	
b.	Sit down with a cup of tea first, but decide to tidy it up before settling down for the evening.	
c.	Leave it, as you are not bothered by living in a mess.	

11. You are involved in a minor road accident and your car gets dented. Do you:

a.	Calmly exchange insurance details with the other driver and make a mental note of the circumstances of the accident.	
b.	Take a note of the other driver's details with shaky hands.	
c.	Fail to do any of the things necessary as you are far too shaken by the accident.	

12. You have just completed an examination. Do you:

score

a.	Forget about it as soon as you get home as the results will not be out for another three months.	
b.	Check a few points when you get home and then lay it to rest.	
c.	Keep thinking about it for some time and wonder how you could have done better.	

13. You have said something embarrassing among a group of friends. Do you:

score

a.	Forget about it as soon as you leave.	
b.	Keep thinking about it but accept that it's too late to worry.	
c.	Lie awake worrying all night.	

14. Some friends have announced they are coming to stay for the weekend. Do you:

score

a.	Feel excited and plan the weekend ahead with enthusiasm.	
b.	Look forward to the weekend but feel rather nervous about whether it will go all right.	
c.	Dread the weekend and think you'll never manage to get everything ready.	

15. You're looking for a book that seems to have been misplaced. Do you:

score

a.	Get irritable and can't relax unless you find the book.	
b.	Keep looking for the book until you have found it.	
c.	Stay calm and decide to look for the book when you've got the time.	

16. You are out shopping and seem to have lost your credit card wallet. Do you:

score

a.	Remain calm and enquire at all the shops whether the cards have been found before telephoning the bank.	
b.	Dash home in a panic to tell your family of the disaster.	
c.	Phone the credit card company to ask what to do.	

17. You are completing an urgent piece of work on your computer when the power goes off. Do you:

score

a.	Take it calmly – you back up your work frequently anyway.	
b.	Lose your temper – it's two hours' work wasted.	
c.	Shrug your shoulders and start again.	

18. You look in the mirror and notice you have put on a lot of weight. Do you:

score

a.	Go on a strict diet and book a course at the gym.	
b.	Relax – your family have always been big.	
c.	Decide to be a bit more careful what you eat.	

19. You are about to go into town and your usual bus has been cancelled. Do you:

score

a.	Think, 'Not to worry, there'll be another one soon.'	
b.	Worry that you'll be late.	
c.	Feel irritated but realize there's nothing you can do.	

20. While driving you witness a road accident. Do you:

score

a.	See if anyone is injured, then phone the emergency services.	
b.	Rush around in a panic until help arrives.	
c.	Ask passers-by if they will help.	

21. You are suffering from aches and pains the origin of which you are unsure of. Do you:

score

a.	Assume that it's a minor problem that will clear up of its own accord.	
b.	Assume you have a serious disease and rush to the doctor.	
c.	Decide to wait and see if your symptoms get worse before taking any action.	

22. A friend turns up unexpectedly for the afternoon. Do you:

score

a.	Drop what you're doing and enjoy his/her company.	
b.	Worry that you will not get your work done.	
c.	Decide to enjoy the social occasion because you can catch up on work later.	

23. You have been called to see your boss for a talk this afternoon and don't know what it's about. Do you:

score

a.	Assume you're being promoted.	
b.	Assume you're in trouble.	
c.	Assume nothing and wait to see what happens.	

24. You are cooking a dinner for a few friends and realize you have forgotten to buy an important ingredient. Do you:

score

a.	Decide that the whole meal is now ruined.	
b.	Decide that no one will notice the oversight.	
c.	Try to replace the ingredient with something different.	

25. You have arranged to meet a friend at an agreed place and seem to have lost your way. Time is running out. Do you:

score

a.	Ask a passer-by for directions.	
b.	Calmly assess where you are and try to decide what route to take.	
c.	Get flustered and rush on madly with little idea of where you are going.	

SCORING

For each answer score the number of points indicated.

1. a:1, b:3, c:2	**10.** a:3, b:2, c:1	**19.** a:1, b:3, c:2
2 a:1, b:2, c:3	**11.** a:1, b:2, c:3	**20.** a:1, b:3, c:2
3. a:1, b:3, c:2	**12.** a:1, b:2, c:3	**21.** a:1, b:3, c:2
4. a:3, b:1, c:2	**13.** a:1, b:2, c:3	**22.** a:1, b:3, c:2
5. a:1, b:2, c:3	**14.** a:1, b:2, c:3	**23.** a:1, b:3, c:2
6. a:1, b:2, c:3	**15.** a:3, b:2, c:1	**24.** a:3, b:1, c:2
7. a:1, b:3, c:2	**16.** a:1, b:3, c:2	**25.** a:1, b:2, c:3
8. a:1, b:3, c:2	**17.** a:1, b:3, c:2	
9. a:3, b:2, c:1	**18.** a:3, b:1, c:2	

The maximum score is 75. If you scored over 65, you are a very anxious person indeed. You should seriously consider ways to calm down and take things more easily. If you scored over 50 but below 64, you are inclined to worry but do not let it get out of control. A score in the 40s would suggest average levels of anxiety (most of the population score in this range). If you scored in the 30s, you are really not much of a worrier at all. A score below 30 would suggest that you are very relaxed, perhaps to the extent that you do not worry much even about things that should probably concern you.

are you an optimist or a pessimist? Do you always carry an umbrella when you go out? Do you just know that things are going to go wrong, or is your life one long round of sunny expectation? Do you assume that things will always turn out all right in the end? Try the following quiz to see how you measure up as an optimist.

1. Do you lock away your valuables when you go away on holiday?

a. Always.   **b.** Usually.   **c.** Never.   **score** ☐

2. If you lost your keys in the supermarket, would you expect them to be returned?

a. No.   **b.** I'd hope so.   **c.** Of course.   **score** ☐

3. Do you believe that your luck will change for the better?

a. Never.   **b.** Sometimes.   **c.** Always.   **score** ☐

4. When the phone rings, do you usually expect bad news?

a. Yes.   **b.** No.   **c.** Sometimes..   **score** ☐

5. Do you buy shares for speculation?

a. Frequently.   **b.** Seldom.   **c.** Never.   **score** ☐

6. Do you believe that the next year will bring success to you?

a. Yes.   **b.** No.   **c.** Don't know.   **score** ☐

7. Do you believe the future will be rosy?

a. No.   **b.** Yes.   **c.** Don't know.   **score** ☐

8. Do you think that most people are honest?

a. No.   **b.** Don't know.   **c.** Yes.   **score** ☐

9. Would you trust an ex-convict?

a. Not sure.   **b.** No.   **c.** Yes.   **score** ☐

10. If it's raining, do you think that it will soon stop?

a. Usually.   **b.** Sometimes.   **c.** Never.   **score** ☐

11. Do you believe that one day you will win the lottery?

score ☐

a. No.   **b.** Yes.   **c.** Not sure.

12. Do you expect to lose some luggage on a long plane flight?

score ☐

a. Yes.   **b.** Uncertain.   **c.** No.

13. Do you bet on horses?

score ☐

a. Never.   **b.** Sometimes. **c.** Often.

14. Do you consider yourself lucky?

a. Usually. **b.** Sometimes. **c.** Seldom   score ☐

15. If you trod on a nail, would you expect it to pierce your foot?

score ☐

a. Yes.   **b.** No.   **c.** Not sure.

16. If you played darts with a friend, would you expect to win?

score ☐

a. Perhaps.   **b.** No.   **c.** Yes.

17. Do you expect your new outfit to be a success?

score ☐

a. Always. **b.** Sometimes. **c.** Never.

18. Do you expect to be sick on a boat?

score ☐

a. Never.   **b.** Always.   **c.** Sometimes.

19. Do you expect it to rain when you play sports?

score ☐

a. Sometimes. **b.** Never.   **c.** Always.

20. Do you expect a burst pipe at some time in winter?

score ☐

a. Yes.   **b.** No.   **c.** Don't know.

21. If you have a glass of beer that is half full, do you consider it to be half empty?

score ☐

a. No.   **b.** Yes.   **c.** Uncertain.

22. If you had a flat, would you hope that somebody would stop and help?

score ☐

a. Not sure.   **b.** Yes.   **c.** No.

23. Do you expect promotion at work?

score ☐

a. Yes.   **b.** Not sure.   **c.** No.

24. If it's cloudy and cold do you expect snow?

score ☐

a. Usually. **b.** Sometimes. **c.** Never.

25. When you plan a barbecue, do you expect it to rain?

a. Yes. **b.** No. **c.** Sometimes. score ☐

26. Do you think that your position at work will improve?

a. Not sure. **b.** No. **c.** Yes. score ☐

27. Do you carry an umbrella in winter?

a. Always. **b.** Sometimes. **c.** Never. score ☐

28. Do you save for a rainy day?

a. Always. **b.** Never thought of it.
c. A bit. score ☐

29. If you car fails to start do you expect a serious defect?

a. Yes. **b.** Not sure. **c.** No. score ☐

30. Do you expect to win at bingo?

a. No. **b.** Yes. **c.** Not sure. score ☐

31. Have you a large life insurance policy?

a. Yes. **b.** I have no policy.
c. Just a small one. score ☐

32. Do you expect to pass every examination?

a. No. **b.** Mostly. **c.** Yes. score ☐

33. If you have an illness, do you expect to recover quickly?

a. Usually. **b.** Sometimes. **c.** No. score ☐

34. Do you expect your bus to be late?

a. Always. **b.** Sometimes. **c.** Never. score ☐

35. Would you select a horse in a race with a pin?

a. Of course. **b.** By no means.
c. I might do. score ☐

36. In winter do you carry a spade in your car?

a. Never. **b.** Sometimes. **c.** Always. score ☐

37. Do you buy raffle tickets?

a. Often. **b.** Never. **c.** Occasionally. score ☐

38. Do you consider that you are more often lucky than unlucky?

a. Yes. **b.** No. **c.** Not sure. score ☐

ARE YOU OPTIMISTIC?

39. Would you take in a stray dog?

score

a. Yes.   **b.** No.   **c.** Not sure.

40. Would you eat a dish that you had never tried before?

score

a. Of course. **b.** Not sure. **c.** Probably not.

41. Will you celebrate the millennium?

score

a. Yes.   **b.** No.   **c.** Unsure.

42. Do you carry a lucky charm?

score

a. Never. **b.** Always. **c.** Sometimes.

43. Are you anticipating a large bonus?

score

a. Unsure.   **b.** No.   **c.** Yes.

44. Do you expect it to rain on your holiday?

score

a . Never. **b.** Sometimes. **c.** Always.

45. Do you expect to be made redundant this year?

score

a. Yes.   **b.** No.   **c.** Unsure.

46. Do you expect the football team that you support will have a good season?

score

a. Of course. **b.** Probably not.
c. I don't know.

47. Would you trust a complete stranger?

score

a. Maybe.   **b.** No.   **c.** Yes.

48. Do you pay a large sum into a pension fund?

score

a. Yes. **b.** No.
c. I only have a small pension.

49. If you drop some money, do you expect to find it all?

score

a. Of course. **b.** Probably not.
c. Unsure.

50. When you plant bulbs, do you expect them all to flower?

score

a. Yes. **b.** Not sure. **c.** Probably not.

100

SCORING KEY

For each answer score the number of points indicated.

1.	a:1, b:2, c:3	**14.**	a:3, b:2, c:1	**27.**	a:1, b:2, c:3	**40.**	a:3, b:2, c:1
2.	a:1, b:2, c:3	**15.**	a:1, b:3, c:2	**28.**	a:1, b:3, c:2	**41.**	a:3, b:1, c:2
3.	a:1, b:2, c:3	**16.**	a:2, b:1, c:3	**29.**	a:1, b:2, c:3	**42.**	a:1, b:3, c:2
4.	a:1, b:3, c:2	**17.**	a:3, b:2, c:1	**30.**	a:1, b:3, c:2	**43.**	a:2, b:1, c.3
5.	a:3, b:2, c:1	**18.**	a:3, b:1, c:2	**31.**	a:1, b:3, c:2	**44.**	a:3, b:2, c:1
6.	a:3, b:1, c:2	**19.**	a:2, b:3, c:1	**32.**	a:1, b:2, c:3	**45.**	a:1, b:3, c:2
7.	a:1, b:3, c:2	**20.**	a:1, b:3, c:2	**33.**	a:3, b:2, c:1	**46.**	a:3, b:1, c:2
8.	a:1, b:2, c:3	**21.**	a:3, b:1, c:2	**34.**	a:1, b:2, c:3	**47.**	a:2, b:1, c:3
9.	a:2, c:1, c:3	**22.**	a:2, b:3, c:1	**35.**	a:3, b:1, c:2	**48.**	a:3, b:1, c:2
10.	a:3, b:2, c:1	**23.**	a:3, b:2, c:1	**36.**	a:3, b:2, c:1	**49.**	a:3, b:1, c:2
11.	a:1, b:3, c:2	**24.**	a:1, b:2, c:3	**37.**	a:3, b:1, c:2	**50.**	a:3, b:2, c:1
12.	a:1, b:2, c:3	**25.**	a:1, b:3, c:2	**38.**	a:3, b:1, c:2		
13.	a:1, b:2, c:3	**26.**	a:2, b:1, c:3	**39.**	a:3, b:1, c:2		

The maximum score is 150. If you scored over 125, you must be in a permanent, and enviable, state of optimism. You look at the world through rose-tinted glasses, and it never occurs to you that things could turn out badly. Even when you do suffer the odd reversal, you consider it a temporary mishap in your otherwise fortunate life. Living with you must be a strain.

If you scored between 100 and 124, you are still a pretty optimistic kind of person, and your world view is generally warm and comfortable. You are aware that life may have its bad patches, but on the whole you don't expect such things to happen to you.

If you scored from 75 to 99, you are quite balanced in your outlook. You don't expect too much of life, but on the other hand you're not exactly gloomy either. Most people will probably score in this range.

If you scored from 50 to 74, you are rather pessimistic. You don't expect your life to be easy, and feel that on the whole if things can go wrong, they will.

If you scored below 50, why bother to get out of bed? Your life is not worth living and you never really thought that it would be.

1. The time has come to book the next summer holiday. Would you decide on:

score

a.	A stay in a gite in the French countryside.	
b.	Hiring a villa in a Greek seaside resort with a group of friends.	
c.	An all-inclusive holiday in a Spanish holiday village with all-day sports and entertainment.	

2. You have a couple of hours to spare in the afternoon. Do you:

score

a.	Phone a friend who lives nearby and invite him/her over for a coffee.	
b.	Catch up on some household chores that you have neglected for ages.	
c.	Have a lie down on your bed with a novel.	

3. You are asked by your boss to take a new business contact out to lunch. Do you:

score

a.	Look forward to the meeting and the discussion over lunch.	
b.	Dread it and wish it was already over.	
c.	Regard it as part of the job but without much enthusiasm.	

4. A new couple moves in next door. Do you:

score

a.	Try to catch them on their way out and introduce yourself.	
b.	Knock on their door the first evening and invite them over for a glass of wine.	
c.	Wait until you bump into them to say hello.	

5. A friend invites you to her party where you will only know very few people. Do you:

score

a.	Look forward to the chance of meeting some new people.	
b.	Tell her you are busy that evening and invite her around on her own on a different evening instead.	
c.	Go to the party but mainly talk to the few people you already know.	

6. A friend suggests joining a social club in your village. Would you:

		score
a.	Tell her you are far too busy as you hate joining any kind of club.	
b.	Join the club to keep her company but secretly wish you did not have to go.	
c.	Tell her what a wonderful idea it is and how much you would enjoy getting to know other people in the village.	

7. You are looking for a new job. Would you consider a position that involves:

		score
a.	Going abroad frequently with a team of colleagues.	
b.	Working on your own on a project that has fascinated you for a long time.	
c.	Working in a small office in liaison with a few other colleagues.	

8. After a forecast predicting rain for the weekend, the weather has turned out better than expected. Do you:

		score
a.	Spend the day decorating the living room as planned.	
b.	Go out for a long walk instead and do a bit of decorating later in the day.	
c.	Postpone decorating and try to book a hotel at the seaside on the spur of the moment.	

9. On your way to the postbox a neighbor is walking toward you on the opposite side of the road. Do you:

		score
a.	Walk across the road and make a comment on the weather.	
b.	Stay on the same side of the road and give a weak smile.	
c.	Stop and have a 15-minute chat.	

10. On a Sunday morning you ideally:

		score
a.	Have a long lie in.	
b.	Go to the gym for a workout.	
c.	Do jobs around the house.	

11. You are to attend a meeting where an important issue is at stake. Do you:

		score
a.	Sit down and make a detailed list of the points you might raise.	
b.	Have a think one hour before the meeting about what you might say.	
c.	Go into the meeting unprepared and take part in the discussion as you go along.	

12. You move to a new area. Do you:

		score
a.	Join a local club and take up a new hobby.	
b.	Join an evening class to carry on with your studies in French.	
c.	Decide you are too busy to join anything but carry on seeing a few friends from your previous location.	

13. You are offered a high-paid job building up a company that has been in existence for only three months. Do you:

		score
a.	Jump at the chance of the new challenge lying ahead of you.	
b.	Stick with the familiarity of the job you have had for the past few years – the new job's prospects sound far too risky to you.	
c.	Keep looking for a job with a more established company, though you would have loved the change.	

14. You go to a meeting at your children's school. Do you:

		score
a.	Enthuse about the chance to discuss various issues with a group of parents.	
b.	Listen to what the other parents have to say but do not feel you could make a contribution yourself.	
c.	Throw in the occasional comment.	

15. You have decided to do some charity Do you choose to:

a.	Sort out clothes donations in a local charity shop.	
b.	Carry out door-to-door collections.	
c.	Arrange and hold fund-raising activities.	

16. Christmas is coming up in one month's time. work. You:

score

a.	Bought and wrapped up all your presents four weeks earlier.	
b.	Are looking through catalogues for gift ideas.	
c.	Leave all the shopping until the weekend before Christmas.	

17. A friend tells you a person close to her is suffering from a terminal illness. Do you:

score

a.	Get terribly upset and think of nothing else all day.	
b.	Listen with sympathy and comfort your friend.	
c.	Listen politely but with detachment – after all, she is not a personal friend of yours.	

18. For the third time in a row your partner has come home late from work without phoning you, and again the dinner is ruined. Do you:

score

a.	Lose your temper, shout at him the moment he gets in and ask him to get himself a take-away if he wants to eat.	
b.	Not show him you are angry but tell him rationally that it would really be better to phone.	
c.	Show him you're annoyed and make it clear that this is the last meal you have wasted.	

ARE YOU AN EXTROVERT?

105

19. You have been doing the same job for 10 years and feel fed up. Do you:

		score
a.	Hand in your notice on the spur of the moment because you cannot stand it any longer.	
b.	Buy the local paper and browse through the job ads.	
c.	Persevere with the job as it is well paid and familiar to you.	

20. A relative unexpectedly cancels an invitation for Saturday night. Do you:

		score
a.	Invite a few close friends to a dinner party.	
b.	Go to a lively dance at your local community centre.	
c.	Hire a video.	

21. You are trying to find an address but seem to have lost your way. You haven't got a map. Do you:

		score
a.	Walk back to the point you set out from and start again.	
b.	Ask the next person you come across for directions.	
c.	Buy a chocolate bar in a newsagents further down the road and ask the shop assistant for the way.	

22. You have decided to start exercising. Do you:

		score
a.	Join a local sports team.	
b.	Go jogging before breakfast.	
c.	Play tennis with a friend.	

23. You are planning a day out. Do you choose to:

		score
a.	Go to an amusement park and go on lots of white-knuckle rides.	
b.	Spend a relaxing day on the beach.	
c.	Go to a leisure pool with slides and other water features.	

24. A morning of household chores lies ahead of you. Do you:

		score
a.	Get them done as quickly as possible so that you can get on with other things.	
b.	Do them at a leisurely pace with a cup of coffee halfway through.	
c.	Do them thoroughly but without stopping in between.	

25. A public figure you admired has been killed. Do you:

		score
a.	Wonder what all the fuss is about – after all he was not personally known to you.	
b.	Watch his funeral on television crying your eyes out.	
c.	Attend the public funeral and join other mourners in their grief.	

26. After Sunday lunch you have an hour to spare. Do you choose to:

		score
a.	Take a nap.	
b.	Do some work in the garden.	
c.	Phone friends for a chat.	

27. You decide to spend the evening watching television. Would you watch:

		score
a.	A concert.	
b.	A current affairs documentary.	
c.	A game show.	

28. You are taking part in a planning meeting on new projects for the future. Are you:

		score
a.	Full of ideas about the overall project.	
b.	Keen on devising ways of carrying out the project.	
c.	Able to throw in suggestions on both aspects.	

29. You are offered the chance of a trip abroad the following weekend. Do you:

score

a.	Accept it immediately without hesitation.	
b.	Say you would love to go but you need to check first about any previous engagements with your partner.	
c.	Weigh up carefully the pros and cons of the trip before making up your mind.	

30. You are enquiring about a holiday property. Do you:

score

a.	Phone the owners and ask them to send you a brochure.	
b.	Write to the owners for some information.	
c.	Phone the owners for information and discuss your requirements with them.	

31. You are on your way to do your weekly shopping. Do you:

score

a.	Go with a shopping list but allow yourself to be tempted to buy other items.	
b.	Only buy items that are on your shopping list as you could otherwise not keep any control over your spending.	
c.	Decide what to buy when you are in the store and worry about the shopping bill later.	

32. You are shopping in town and see an expensive dress that you would love to have. Do you:

score

a.	Buy it on the spur of the moment.	
b.	Decide to think it over when you get home and possibly buy it the next time you are in town.	
c.	Think about it while finishing the rest of the shopping and then go back for it.	

33. It's Friday and you have not made any arrangements for Saturday yet. Do you:

score

a.	Watch the weather forecast and plan out exactly what you want to do with your time off.	
b.	Decide on the day when you know what sort of mood you are in.	
c.	Have some ideas but do not make any firm plans.	

34. You are in a train reading a newspaper when another passenger sits down in your compartment. Do you:

score

a.	Ignore the person and carry on reading your paper.	
b.	Look up briefly, say hello and then bury your head in the paper again.	
c.	Try starting a conversation.	

35. An acquaintance asks you to carry out a door-to-door collection for a good cause. Do you:

score

a.	Agree to do it with enthusiasm as it seems a good way of raising money.	
b.	Decline politely as you hate knocking on strangers' doors asking for money.	
c.	Agree to it as you find it difficult to say no.	

36. You have to make a speech on a social occasion. Do you:

score

a.	Write it out beforehand and learn it by heart.	
b.	Make a few notes on the points you want to address.	
c.	Improvise when the occasion arises.	

37. You are asked to sign a credit agreement. Do you:

score

a.	Decide to take it home and read it through quietly before signing anything.	
b.	Sign immediately as the sales consultant has explained everything you feel you need to know.	
c.	Read the agreement through carefully, including the small print, and then sign it in the store.	

38. You meet somebody you know by sight on a bus and he starts a conversation with you. Do you:

score

a.	Feel uncomfortable because you do not know what to talk about.	
b.	Make a few polite comments so as not to appear unsociable.	
c.	Feel happy to have met somebody to pass the time with on the bus journey.	

39. You are thinking of booking a weekend break. Would you consider:

		score
a.	A horse-riding weekend with a group of strangers.	
b.	A multi-sports weekend with a close friend.	
c.	A stay in a seaside cottage with your partner.	

40. You are attending a large office party. Do you:

		score
a.	Talk to a wide variety of people and tend to dominate the conversation.	
b.	Talk predominantly to the people you work with and know well.	
c.	Tend to stay in the background and only make the odd remark.	

41. You are invited to a talk about possible life in space followed by a discussion session. Do you:

		score
a.	Accept the invitation with anticipation.	
b.	Go to the talk as you have not got anything better to do.	
c.	Decline the invitation and go to your local pub instead.	

42. You are in the company of a few friends. Do you prefer to:

		score
a.	Have a serious discussion on a subject of interest.	
b.	Crack some jokes and have a good laugh.	
c.	Talk about some everyday matters.	

43. You are working on a project. Do you:

		score
a.	Pay attention to all the details and double-check everything you write.	
b.	Place the importance on the broad issues of the project, as details are unimportant.	
c.	Write steadily and read it through to eliminate any obvious mistakes once when you have finished .	

44. Christmas is on your doorstep. Do you look forward to:

		score
a.	A quiet few days spent with your family.	
b.	The opportunity to see a few close friends during the period.	
c.	The chance to go to some lively Christmas parties.	

45. The weather is awful and you are faced with a Sunday morning reading the paper. Do you:

		score
a.	Feel delighted that for once you have a chance for a good read.	
b.	Hate the idea of sitting around all morning.	
c.	Read the paper for a while but then occupy yourself with a few jobs.	

46. Your partner tells you it's time to invite some friends and colleagues to a party at your home. Are you:

		score
a.	Full of enthusiasm and look forward to organizing the event.	
b.	Nervous at the prospect, but feel it is your duty to do it.	
c.	Keen to convince your partner that it can really wait for a bit longer.	

47. A couple of friends phone up and ask if they could stay with you for a week. Do you:

		score
a.	Tell them you just haven't got enough space, as you cannot bear the thought of having somebody staying for that long.	
b.	Invite them to stay as you do not want to hurt their feelings.	
c.	Look forward to having constant company for a week.	

48. You are told by your boss that you will have to do a lot of foreign travelling within the next few months. Do you:

		score
a.	Love the idea of seeing new places and meeting new people.	
b.	Quite like the idea but do not enjoy being away from your family.	
c.	Dread the prospect of letting go of your routine.	

ARE YOU AN EXTROVERT?

49. You are offered a summer job organizing entertainment in a holiday village. Do you:

		score
a.	Grasp the opportunity as the job should be fun and you are bound to meet lots of people.	
b.	Take the job as nothing better has come up.	
c.	Decline the offer as you would hate a job where you are constantly surrounded by people.	

50. A friend asks you to accompany her to a pottery class for the first time. Do you:

		score
a.	Go with her just to be helpful.	
b.	Tell her you do not want to go as you have never done pottery before.	
c.	Love the idea of trying out something new	

SCORING KEY

For each answer score the number of points indicated.

1.	a:1, b:2, c:3	**14.**	a:3, b:1, c:2	**27.**	a:1, b:2, c:3	**40.**	a:3, b:2, c:1
2.	a:3, b:2, c:1	**15.**	a:1, b:2, c:3	**28.**	a:3, b:2, c:1	**41.**	a:3, b:2, c:1
3.	a:3, b:1, c:2	**16.**	a:1, b:3, c:2	**29.**	a:2, b:1, c:3	**42.**	a:1, b:3, c:2
4.	a:2, b:3, c:1	**17.**	a:3, b:2, c:1	**30.**	a:2, b:1, c:3	**43.**	a:1, b:3, c:2
5.	a:3, b:1, c:2	**18.**	a:3, b:1, c:2	**31.**	a:3, b:1, c:2	**44.**	a:1, b:2, c:3
6.	a:1, b:2, c:3	**19.**	a:3, b:2, c:1	**32.**	a:1, b:3, c:2	**45.**	a:1, b:3, c2
7.	a:3, b:1, c:2	**20.**	a:2, b:3, c:1	**33.**	a:1, b:2, c:3	**46.**	a:3, b:2, c:1
8.	a:1, b:2, c:3	**21.**	a:1, b:3, c:2	**34.**	a:3, b:1, c:2	**47.**	a:1, b:2, c:3
9.	a:2, b:1, c:3	**22.**	a:3, b:1, c:2	**35.**	a:3, b:1, c:2	**48.**	a:3, b:2, c:1
10.	a:1, b:3, c:2	**23.**	a:3, b:1, c:2	**36.**	a:1, b:2, c:3	**49.**	a:3, b:2, c:1
11.	a:1, b:2, c:3	**24.**	a:3, b:1, c:2	**37.**	a:1, b:3, c:2	**50.**	a:2, b:1, c:3
12.	a:3, b:2, c:1	**25.**	a:1, b:2, c:3	**38.**	a:1, b:2, c:3		
13.	a:3, b:1, c:2	**26.**	a:1, b:2, c:3	**39.**	a:3, b:2, c:1		

Over 125

The maximum score is 150. Anything over 125 would suggest that you are extremely extrovert. Your main love is communicating with other people and you feel lonely and uncomfortable when confronted with solitary tasks. You are also socially bold and enjoy taking risks. Your idea of hell is an evening spent alone with a good book.

100–124

If you scored between 100 and 124, you are still quite extrovert but are not so dependent on other people that you suffer withdrawal symptoms when left alone.

75–99

If your score was between 75 and 99, you are average. You enjoy company but can easily spend time alone and enjoy that too. You are by no means cautious but you feel no compulsion to take risks or to involve yourself in situations where the spotlight is upon you.

50–74

If you scored between 50 and 74, you are quite introverted and on the whole prefer to keep away from social situations. You find that you are most at ease when allowed to get on with solitary tasks.

Below 50

If you scored below 50, you are really very introverted and find the society of others stressful. You will happily work alone and, if allowed to do so, will also spend your leisure hours in quiet pursuits.

it is hard to decide what a question like 'How religious are you?' might mean. Religion means so many different things to different people and, if you examine the subject globally, you quickly discover religious concepts in one culture that would be incomprehensible in another. As this book is written primarily for a British and American audience we decided that, for the purposes of this test only, we would consider 'religious' to refer to a traditional, fundamentalist belief in one God as revealed to us through the Scriptures. This is a view that should also be familiar to, even if not accepted by, Jewish and Muslim readers. A high score on this test would indicate a firm belief in traditional religious values.

1. Are you a member of any established religion?
a. Yes. **b.** No. **c.** In name only. **score** ☐

2. Do you believe that prayers are answered?
a. Always. **b.** Sometimes. **c.** Never.
score ☐

3. Do you believe that morality is divinely inspired?
a. No. **b.** Yes. **c.** Don't know. **score** ☐

4. Do you believe that we are punished for our sins?
a. Don't know. **b.** Yes. **c.** No. **score** ☐

5. Do you believe that virtue is its own reward?
a. No. **b.** Yes. **c.** Don't know. **score** ☐

6. Do you believe in life after death?
a. Yes. **b.** No. **c.** Don't know. **score** ☐

7. Do you believe that the world was created by God?
a. No. **b.** Yes. **c.** Don't know. **score** ☐

8. Do you believe that our actions are noted by God?
a. Don't know. **b.** Yes. **c.** No. **score** ☐

9. Do you believe in evil as an entity?
a. No. **b.** Yes. **c.** Don't know. **score** ☐

10. Can illness be cured by religious faith?
a. Yes. **b.** No. **c.** Don't know. **score** ☐

11. Do you believe that miracles occur?
a. Don't know. **b.** Yes. **c.** No. **score** ☐

12. Do you believe that God intervenes in the world?
a. No. **b.** Yes. **c.** Don't know. **score** ☐

13. Do you attend a place of worship?
a. Frequently. **b.** Occasionally. **c.** Never. **score** ☐

14. Do you believe that your life has been benefited by religion?
a. Yes. **b.** Unsure. **c.** No. **score** ☐

15. Do you consider the religious implications of the way you act in daily life?
a. Always. **b.** Never. **c.** Usually. **score** ☐

16. How important is religion in your life?
a. Not important. **b.** Very important.
c. Quite important. **score** ☐

17. Do you consider that there is only one true religion?
a. Unsure. **b.** Yes. **c.** No. **score** ☐

18. Do you read religious texts?
a. Often. **b.** Sometimes. **c.** Never. **score** ☐

19. Would you like the life of a priest, vicar, rabbi, etc?
a. Yes. **b.** No. **c.** Don't know. **score** ☐

20. Could you live without your religious faith?
a. Unsure. **b.** No. **c.** Yes. **score** ☐

21. Do you look to God for guidance in your life?
a. Always. **b.** Sometimes. **c.** Never. **score** ☐

22. Do you believe that science and religion are incompatible?
a. No. **b.** Yes. **c.** Unsure. **score** ☐

23. Does religious faith give you courage in difficult situations?
a. Always. **b.** Sometimes. **c.** Never. **score** ☐

24. Do you stick strictly to the tenets of your religion?
a. Rigidly. **b.** Not rigidly.
c. I'm quite lax about them. **score** ☐

25. Do you have doubts about the existence of God?
a. Never. **b.** Sometimes. **c.** Always. **score** ☐

26. Do you ever doubt the teachings of your religious organization?
a. Often. **b.** Sometimes. **c.** Never. **score** ☐

27. Would a serious misfortune persuade you to abandon your religion?
a. No. **b.** Yes. **c.** Unsure. **score**

28. Do you believe that there will be a day of judgement for all of us?
a. Yes. **b.** No. **c.** Don't know. **score**

29. Do you see the hand of God in everyday events?
a. No. **b.** Yes. **c.** Unsure. **score**

30. Would you be prepared to suffer for your faith?
a. Unsure. **b.** No. **c.** Yes. **score**

31. Would you be prepared to die for your faith?
a. Yes. **b.** Unsure. **c.** No. **score**

32. Is your religion the most important thing in your life?
a. Yes. **b.** No **c.** Unsure. **score**

33. Would you be prepared for your child to marry someone of another faith?
a. Unsure. **b.** No. **c.** Yes. **score**

34. Would you consider marrying outside your religion?
a. Yes. **b.** No. **c.** Unsure **score**

35. Do you approve of interfaith marriage for other people?
a. No. **b.** Yes. **c.** Unsure. **score**

36. Do you socialize with people outside your faith?
a. Often. **b.** Never. **c.** Sometimes. **score**

37. Do you know much about other religions?
a. A lot. **b.** Not much. **c.** Nothing. **score**

38. Do you believe comparative religion should be taught in schools?
a. Unsure. **b.** No. **c.** Yes. **score**

39. Do you feel that your children should be taught about religion in school?
a. Yes. **b.** No. **c.** Unsure **score**

40. Would you let your children go to a school where other religions are taught?
a. No. **b.** Unsure. **c.** Yes. **score**

41. Would you send your children to a religious school if one were available?
a. No. **b.** Yes. **c.** Unsure. **score**

42. Could you accept a member of your family converting to another religion?
a. Yes. **b.** No. **c.** Unsure. **score**

43. Can you work happily alongside members of other faiths?
a. No. **b.** Unsure. **c.** Yes. **score** ☐

44. Do you bring your beliefs into conversations with people you meet in your daily life?
a. Often. **b.** Sometimes. **c.** Never. **score** ☐

45. Do you try to convert others to your beliefs?
a. Sometimes. **b.** Often. **c.** Never. **score** ☐

46. Do you believe that members of other religions (or none) are damned?
a. Yes. **b.** No **c.** Unsure. **score** ☐

47. Would you listen to someone who tried to convert you to another religion?
a. Yes. **b.** No. **c.** Unsure. **score** ☐

48. Do you approve of sex other than for the purpose of procreation?
a. No. **b.** Unsure. **c.** Yes. **score** ☐

49. Do you feel that most people are sinful?
a. Unsure. **b.** No. **c.** Yes. **score** ☐

50. Do you feel that moral values are not possible without religion?
a. Yes. **b.** No. **c.** Unsure. **score** ☐

SCORING KEY

For each answer score the number of points indicated.

1. a:1, b:3, c:2	**8.** a:3, b:1, c:2	**15.** a:1, b:3, c:2	**22.** a:3, b:1, c:2
2. a:1, b:3, c:2	**9.** a:1, b:3, c:2	**16.** a:1, b:2, c:3	**23.** a:1, b:2, c:3
3. a:1, b:2, c:3	**10.** a:3, b:1, c:2	**17.** a:2, b:1, c:3	**24.** a:2, b:3, c:1
4. a:1, b:2, c:3	**11.** a:2, b:1, c:3	**18.** a:3, b:1, c:2	**25.** a:1, b:3, c:2
5. a:3, b:1, c:2	**12.** a:3, b:2, c:1	**19.** a:2, b:1, c:3	
6. a:2, b:3, c:1	**13.** a:1, b:3, c:2	**20.** a:3, b:1, c:2	
7. a:1, b:3, c:2	**14.** a:1, b:3, c:2	**21.** a:2, b:1, c:3	

SCORING

Over 125

Maximum score is 150. If you scored over 125, you are a religious traditionalist with no time for doubts, modern views, or anyone's opinions but those of your own faith. This may not be a popular position but, as you see your life being entirely guided by the will of God, you are not likely to care what others may think.

100–124

If you scored between 100 and 124, you are still very much influenced by traditional values but are not completely hidebound in your views. You may even allow yourself to have doubts occasionally, though in the long run you are unlikely to lose your faith.

75–99

If you scored between 75 and 99, you are less traditional in your outlook but religion still plays an important part in your life. You are prepared to admit that religious issues are far from simple and you might well contemplate views other than your own.

50–74

If you scored between 50 and 74, you are not much of a traditionalist and, in fact, you may well have considerable reservations about some religious teachings and practices.

25–49

A score between 25 and 49 would suggest that you have serious doubts about the value of traditional religious beliefs and would not describe yourself as 'religious' as we have defined the term.

Below 25

A score below 25 suggests that you have little interest in the subject and, when you do consider religious matters, you are extremely sceptical on most points. You certainly don't consider yourself to be a religious person in the traditional sense and you probably have little time for those who do.

Some people seem able to cope with just about any eventuality. Left alone on a desert island they would build a house, catch their own food, and probably find a way of attracting rescuers. Others would simply huddle under a palm tree and hope for the best. Where do you come on this scale? The following questions are designed to sort out the practical, 'I can turn my hand to anything' types from the hopelessly helpless. In these days of sexual equality I have deliberately made no distinction between tasks more usually carried out by one sex or another. My position is that to be regarded as really practical today, you should be able to build a brick wall or bake a cake with equal ease.

1. Can you do woodwork repairs?
a. Easily.   **b.** With difficulty.
c. Couldn't cope.   **score** ☐

2. Can you repair a window?
a. Easily.   **b.** With difficulty.
c. Couldn't cope.   **score** ☐

3. Can you look after children?
a. Easily.   **b.** With difficulty.
c. Couldn't cope.   **score** ☐

4. Are you a good gardener?
a. Yes. **b.** Not bad. **c.** No. **score** ☐

5. Can you mend a fuse?
a. Easily.   **b.** With difficulty.
c. Couldn't cope.   **score** ☐

6. Can you organize an office?
a. Easily.   **b.** With difficulty.
c. Couldn't cope.   **score** ☐

7. Can you repair a car?
a. Easily.   **b.** With difficulty.
c. Couldn't cope.   **score** ☐

8. Can you replace a tap washer?
a. Easily.   **b.** With difficulty.
c. Couldn't cope.   **score** ☐

9. Can you provide first aid?
a. Easily.   **b.** With difficulty.
c. Couldn't cope.   **score** ☐

10. Can you remove a bee sting?
a. Easily.   **b.** With difficulty.
c. Couldn't cope.   **score** ☐

11. Can you decorate a room?

a. Easily.   **b.** With difficulty.

c. Couldn't cope.   **score** ☐

12. Can you change a flat?

a. Easily.   **b.** With difficulty.

c. Couldn't cope.   **score** ☐

13. Can you wash clothes?

a. Easily.   **b.** With difficulty.

c. Couldn't cope.   **score** ☐

14. Can you cook a three-course meal?

a. Easily.   **b.** With difficulty.

c. Couldn't cope.   **score** ☐

15. Can you decorate a Christmas tree?

a. Easily.   **b.** With difficulty.

c. Couldn't cope.   **score** ☐

16. Can you lay a patio?

a. Easily.   **b.** With difficulty.

c. Couldn't cope.   **score** ☐

17. Can you pilot a plane?

a. Easily.   **b.** With difficulty.

c. Couldn't cope.   **score** ☐

18. Can you French-polish a table?

a. Easily.   **b.** With difficulty.

c. Couldn't cope.   **score** ☐

19. Can you grow vegetables successfully?

a. Easily.   **b.** With difficulty.

c. Couldn't cope.   **score** ☐

20. Can you knit?

a. Easily.   **b.** With difficulty.

c. Couldn't cope.   **score** ☐

21. Can you repair a computer?

a. Easily.   **b.** With difficulty.

c. Couldn't cope.   **score** ☐

22. Can you drive a large van?

a. Easily.   **b.** With difficulty.

c. Couldn't cope.   **score** ☐

23. Can you solve crossword puzzles?

a. Easily.   **b.** With difficulty.

c. Couldn't cope.   **score** ☐

24. Can you understand the layout of a central heating system?

a. Easily.   **b.** With difficulty.

c. Couldn't cope.   **score** ☐

25. Can you operate a video recorder?

a. Easily.   **b.** With difficulty.

c. Couldn't cope.   **score** ☐

26. Can you dance a tango?

a. Easily.   **b.** With difficulty.

c. Couldn't cope.   **score** ☐

27. Can you drive a car?

a. Easily. **b.** With difficulty.

c. Couldn't cope. **score** ☐

28. Can you mend broken toys?

a. Easily. **b.** With difficulty.

c. Couldn't cope. **score** ☐

29. Can you darn a sock?

a. Easily. **b.** With difficulty.

c. Couldn't cope. **score** ☐

30. Can you climb ladders?

a. Easily. **b.** With difficulty.

c. Couldn't cope. **score** ☐

31. Can you replace a flat battery on a car?

a. Easily. **b.** With difficulty.

c. Couldn't cope. **score** ☐

32. Can you ride a bicycle?

a. Easily. **b.** With difficulty.

c. Couldn't cope. **score** ☐

33. Can you water ski?

a. Easily. **b.** With difficulty.

c. Couldn't cope. **score** ☐

34. Can you ride a horse?

a. Easily. **b.** With difficulty.

c. Couldn't cope. **score** ☐

35. Can you play a sport up to club standard?

a. Easily. **b.** With difficulty.

c. Couldn't cope. **score** ☐

36. Can you fill in your tax return without a mistake?

a. Easily. **b.** With difficulty.

c. Couldn't cope. **score** ☐

37. Can you climb a tall tree?

a. Easily. **b.** With difficulty.

c. Couldn't cope. **score** ☐

38. Can you repair defective gutters?

a. Easily. **b.** With difficulty.

c. Couldn't cope. **score** ☐

39. Can you build a brick wall?

a. Easily. **b.** With difficulty.

c. Couldn't cope. **score** ☐

40. Can you repair a broken vase?

a. Easily. **b.** With difficulty.

c. Couldn't cope. **score** ☐

41. Can you understand the electrical circuitry of your house?

a. Easily. **b.** With difficulty.

c. Couldn't cope. **score** ☐

42. Can you ride a motorcycle?

a. Easily.　　　　　**b.** With difficulty.

c. Couldn't cope.　　**score** ☐

43. Can you erect a shelf?

a. Easily.　　　　　**b.** With difficulty.

c. Couldn't cope.　　**score** ☐

44. Can you paint a house to a professional standard?

a. Easily.　　　　　**b.** With difficulty.

c. Couldn't cope.　　**score** ☐

45. Can you a lay a concrete path?

a. Easily.　　　　　**b.** With difficulty.

c. Couldn't cope.　　**score** ☐

46. Can you replace a broken roof tile?

a. Easily.　　　　　**b.** With difficulty.

c. Couldn't cope.　　**score** ☐

47. Can you iron clothes?

a. Easily.　　　　　**b.** With difficulty.

c. Couldn't cope.　　**score** ☐

48. Can you lay a carpet expertly?

a. Easily.　　　　　**b.** With difficulty.

c. Couldn't cope.　　**score** ☐

49. Can you lay a lawn using grass seed?

a. Easily.　　　　　**b.** With difficulty.

c. Couldn't cope.　　**score** ☐

50. Can you speak a second language?

a. Fluently.　　　　**b.** To school standard.

c. Not at all.　　　**score** ☐

SCORING

For every (a) answer give yourself 3 points, for every (b) answer give yourself 2 points , and for every (c) answer give yourself 0 points.

Over 125

The maximum score is 150. This is a really tough test and to get a high score you would have to be multi-talented. Anything over 125 is really impressive. You're the sort of person who will cope in just about any circumstances. You are practical, capable and indispensable. I hate you.

100–124

Between 100 and 124 you are still quite a practical person and are likely to be able to turn your hand to many important tasks. However, there are some things that are beyond you. At least this makes you human.

75–99

Between 75 and 99 you are only average at practical matters, and although you are by no means helpless, you will often have to seek professional advice.

50–74

If you scored between 50 and 74, you are obviously not very practical. Although you can turn your hand to a few tasks, you generally prefer to rely on others to do these things for you.

Below 50

If your score was below 50, you are really not cut out for practical tasks at all. In fact, you must be extremely popular with all the tradesmen in your locality as you are the sort of person who keeps them in work. Well, someone has to.

people's attitudes to money vary enormously. Some of us let it run right through our fingers while others are happy to spend freely. What about you? Do you reach the end of the month with cash to spare, or are you always on the run from the bank manager? Do you give generously, or is getting money from you like squeezing blood from a stone? This test will find out.

1. Do you darn socks (or get your partner to do so)?

a. Sometimes.   **b.** Always.   **c.** Never.

score ☐

2. About how much do you spend on new clothes each year?

a. $1,500+   **b.** $750+   **c.** $200+

score ☐

3. How often do you have your car serviced?

a. Every three months

b. Every six months.

c. Only when something goes wrong.

score ☐

4. Do you:

a. Buy a car and run it till it falls to bits.

b. Change your car fairly regularly.

c. Change your car every year without fail.

score ☐

5. Do you:

a. Inspect your home regularly to see if anything needs repairing.

b. Only fix things that are actually broken.

c. Keep a casual watch on the state of repairs.

score ☐

6. Do you save scraps of soap and stick them onto each new block that you buy?

a. Never.   **b.** Sometimes.   **c.** Always.

score ☐

7. Do you ever buy clothes, etc. from thrift shops?

a. Often.   **b.** Never.   **c.** Sometimes.

score ☐

8. Do you buy your cars second-hand?

a. Always.   **b.** Sometimes.   **c.** Never.

score ☐